RAVI SHANKER KAPOOR did BA (Hons) Mathematics from Hansraj College, Delhi University, in 1985. He has worked with *The Asian Age, The Financial Express,* and *MetroNow.* Currently, he is working with *The Political and Business Daily.*

He has presently written two hard-hitting books, *More Equal Than Others: A Study of the Indian Left* and *Failing the Promise: Irrelevance of the Vajpayee Government*, both published by Vision Books. He is the first self-proclaimed conservative of India. As a member of the Centre for National Renaissance, he started www.indiaright.org, India's first conservative website

He can be reached at: raviskapoor@gmail.com

How India's Intellectuals Spread Lies

Ravi Shanker Kapoor

For V.

Neend uski hai, dimaagh uska hai, raatein uski hain
Teri zulfien jiski baazu per parishaan ho gaeen

www.vision**books**india.com

First Published, 2007
Reprinted, 2008
Revised and Enlarged Edition, 2015

ISBN 10: 81-7094-917-3
ISBN 13: 978-81-7094-917-6

Published by
Vision Books Pvt. Ltd.
(Incorporating Orient Paperbacks and CARING imprints)
24 Feroze Gandhi Road, Lajpat Nagar 3
New Delhi 110024, India.
Phone: (+91-11) 2984 0821 / 22
e-mail: visionbooks@gmail.com

Printed at
Anand Sons
C-88, Ganesh Nagar, Pandav Nagar Complex
Delhi-110092, India

Contents

Introduction

When the results of the 14th general elections were announced on May 13, 2004, unexpectedly unseating the Atal Bihari Vajpayee government, communist leaders screamed that the verdict was against economic reforms. As an echo effect, our great liberals and intellectuals started shouting: the mandate is against liberalization.

Nobody was willing to have a hard look at the preposterous claim; nobody asked the simple question: have the people voted against reforms? The answer would have been unambiguous: the verdict might have been against anything, it was definitely not against reforms. Simple arithmetic could have proved that the opponents of liberalization were a small minority with a big noise-making capacity—the Leftists. The Congress got 145 seats and the Bharatiya Janata Party 138; the total was 283 Lok Sabha seats, 11 more than the magic figure of 272. And if we include the alliance partners, both alliances put together crossed the 400-mark—that is, about three-fourths of the Lok Sabha members had faith in the acceleration of reforms.

Essentially, it was just the 67-odd Left Front members who were, and are, against reforms. But the entire intellectual class accepted the Leftist lie as gospel truth—and started repeating it *ad nauseum*. This helped the Left in creating a climate of opinion against reforms and even reversing some of them, like the privatization policy.

As for the relationship between reforms and the electoral verdict, both the principal political parties, the Congress and the BJP, had promised in their manifestos that they would speed up reforms. Both had agreed to accelerate economic growth rate, encourage domestic and foreign investment, and even privatize public sector undertakings. Of course, the manifestos were not identical; there were some differences between the two, but the differences were in nuances and tones rather than of basics; essentially, the two manifestos were quite similar. For instance, the NDA aimed at 8-10 per cent growth rate "on a sustainable basis over the next five years, with eradication of poverty by 2001." The Congress' "over-riding objective" was also 8-10 per cent rate of economic growth" spread over all sectors. Similarly, the NDA wanted to carry forward liberalization by rationalizing the tax system, consolidating public sector banks, revising FDI limit in insurance, continuing disinvestment, and so on. The Congress, too, pledged to "broaden and deepen economic reforms."

But our great intellectuals ignored these facts and blindly accepted the Leftist lie that the people had voted against liberalization. Such blind acceptance was not for the first time, neither for the last. Intellectuals seem to have made a tryst with mendacity. They keep mouthing Leftist untruths *ad nauseum*, often without realizing that these are lies. Like the sheep in George Orwell's *Animal Farm*, they keep parroting Leftist lies, clichés, and platitudes—most of the time without understanding the consequences all these would lead to. They end up in the company of Walter Duranty. A star reporter with *New York Times*, Duranty reported from the Soviet Union when the murderous regimes of Lenin and Stalin were killing people in millions.

Lenin coined an interesting term, "useful idiots," for the Left-leaning and liberal intellectuals like Duranty who blindly and unquestioningly accepted Leftist lies. Typically, Duranty wrote rosy accounts from the Soviet Union when collectivization and purges eliminated millions. Even when 25,000 Ukrainian peasants were dying *every day*, Duranty refused to expose the barbarity of communism. Having accepted the ends-justify-the-means argument, he even condoned communist butchery by saying, "You can't make an omelet without breaking a few eggs." On this a commentator, Mark Y. Herring, remarked, "Those 'eggs' were the heads of men, women and children and those 'few' were tens of millions."

In India, too, we have an army of useful idiots—the eminent liberals who are always genuflecting to the Left. And all of them are honorable men and women, pontificating in newspapers and magazines, sermonizing in seminars and television talk shows. Honorable like Duranty, who went on to win the Pulitzer Prize.

Some of the venerable names in India's public discourse—Jawaharlal Nehru, Arundhati Roy, Khushwant Singh, Kuldip Nayar, P. Chidambaram, Mani Shankar Aiyar, Mushirul Hasan, among others—blindly follow the Left on all important issues. They are the descendants of Gandhari. According to *Mahabharata*, Gandhari had blindfolded herself since her husband, Dhritrashtra, was blind. Now Dhritrashtra's blindness was more than physical; he was also blind to the delinquency of his son, Duryodhan; he refused to recognize the evil of Duryodhan. Dhritrashtra *could* not see evil; Gandhari did not *want* to see evil.

Like Gandhari, liberal intellectuals do not want to see evil, be it the malevolence of socialism or of Islamic terror.

While in many chapters I have shown *how* India's intellectuals (Jawaharlal Nehru, Arundhati Roy, Kuldip Nayar, etc.) sell the Left's lies, I have also tried to show *why* they sell such lies. For instance, the chapters 'Guilt: Weapon of Mass Deception' and 'Tyranny of Decibels' deal with the *why* aspect.

This is not a comprehensive study of Indian liberals and intellectuals; that is, this is not a literary criticism of the works of, say, Arundhati Roy and Khushwant Singh; this is a study of an aspect—the most important aspect—of Indian liberalism: that of liberals blindly and slavishly accepting Leftist ideas.

In this book, I have tried to expose them as the sheep of *Animal Farm*, as useful idiots, as the descendants of Gandhari. It is for the reader to decide to what extent I have succeeded.

I would like to mention that all the intellectuals I have discussed in this book are decent, well-meaning people. Personally, I have nothing against them and this book is not against them; it is against the ideas that they carry and spread; it is *against them as the carriers of lies*.

1 Floating Mass Without the Ballast

American thinker Irving Kristol once described neoconservatives like himself as the "liberals who've been mugged by reality". In India, however, the liberal has insulated himself from any assault of reality. Basking in the affected glory of conventional wisdom and comfortable with the soothing clichés of political correctness, he is blissfully ensconced in his own fantasy land: he is not only deracinated, he also enjoys deracination. The rootlessness of Indian liberals is not akin to that of an ornamental plant in a pot hung by a hook; it is rather similar to that of a floating mass without the ballast, like the hyacinth floating over a lake—the putrid lake of public discourse, in this case. Lacking the ballast, the floating mass moves in whichever direction the wind blows (as in the swinging 1960s, liberals still love 'blowing in the wind'). And since the winds of political correctness are still strong, public discourse is conducted primarily in the Leftist idiom. Not surprisingly, the liberal ends up parroting the slogans and shibboleths of a bygone era.

The Penguin Dictionary of Philosophy defines liberalism as:

> "A set of ideas in social and political thought which emphasizes the value of individuals' rights, and individual freedom of choice and freedom from interference. The role of the state is primarily to protect these rights . . . .

"Liberals have traditionally sought to *limit* the scope of state action and to prefer non-governmental initiatives to governmental ones, where this is feasible . . . .

"In contemporary usage in the United States, 'liberalism' and its cognates are frequently used for political views which favor an increased scope for state action in areas such as education, health care, and social welfare. This is a consequence of the liberal principle that the protection of the individuals' rights is an essential function of government, in combination with an increase in the number of goods and services that are thought of as rights, and an increase in the number of ills and imposition (poverty, illness, negative discrimination, lack of education) that have come to be regarded as violations of rights."

This is a comprehensive and general definition, truer in India than in any Western country; for in India the liberal is more likely to move Leftward than in the West. So, the Indian liberal is also a typical intellectual—that is a person who, while downplaying the importance of empirical evidence, wants to change the world relying solely or primarily on intellect. For common people and even genuine scholars, seeing is believing; for intellectuals, believing is seeing. Once they believe in something, which is usually some Left-leaning ideology, they start viewing the entire world from the spectacles of their faith. Empirical evidence and reason become secondary, or even irrelevant; what matters is the ideology. In the Indian context, there is often little difference between Leftists and liberals. So, in this book, we use the terms "Leftists", "liberal", and "intellectual" almost interchangeably.

Even when the Indian liberal supports economic reforms, on any political issue his response would be little different from that of, say, Harkishan Singh Surjeet, former general secretary of the Communist Party of India (Marxist). Swaminathan Aiyar, a senior journalist and vociferous supporter of economic reforms, is of the opinion that Indian security forces butcher "innocent" Kashmiris. Since it is unfashionable to see terrorism as an Islamist movement, he blindly accepts the Leftist interpretation of the issue. He does not feel any compunction in ascribing to Surjeet's political philosophy; he does not realize that the world of the Left is a seamless web. And it does not occur to Aiyar that one cannot accept the politics of Surjeet and reject his economics; one cannot adopt a few features of socialism and hope to remain a liberal. In order to be a true liberal, one has to reject socialism *in toto*, in all its manifestations and forms, all its slogans and clichés, ideas and ideals. Aiyar, like other liberals in India, does not grasp this simple fact.

But a true liberal Friedrich Hayek detected the meretricious charms of socialism. In 1944, he wrote in *The Road to Serfdom*, "Socialism was embraced by the greater part of the intelligentsia as the apparent heir of the liberal tradition: therefore it is not surprising that to them the idea should appear inconceivable of socialism leading to the opposite of liberty."

The problem of the Indian intellectual is also a problem of the entire nation: Leftist thinking has gone to our bones. An important reason for our inability to shed the socialist mindset is that the Left has hijacked the pro-poor agenda. What are the broad goals of the Left? Removal of poverty, employment for all, food and shelter for all, a just and equitable society, peace, world harmony, universal brotherhood—in short, all that mankind cherishes and hopes for has been made out to be a Leftist ideal. It is another matter that the means suggested by the Left to attain these ideals invariably lead to wastage, corruption, confusion, chaos, and worse.

For instance, how does one remove poverty? Leftist radicals would come up with a package of measures, each of which would lead to a drain on the public exchequer and escalation of corruption. Typically, it would include sops like poverty-alleviation schemes, clichés like empowerment and decentralization, and platitudes pertaining to "growth with equity". How does one increase employment? Set up more public sector undertakings (PSUs), even though they have proved to be a burden on the economy. Shelter for all? Set up monoliths like the Delhi Development Authority, even though such organizations have a great reputation for corruption and a demonstrated record of failure. All such remedies have been tried; they have failed miserably, comprehensively. But those who suggest dismantling of such mechanisms, programs, and structures, are immediately denounced as anti-poor and heartless, or stooges of the World Bank or of the US.

Another problem is that the Indian intellectual lacks the courage of conviction. For instance, even when the champions of the Economic Right—who are invariably liberals such as Swaminathan Aiyar—do garner the courage to challenge socialist measures, they don't do it on the grounds that they are bad in principle, as true liberals like Hayek and Milton Friedman do; they oppose such measures because these are "not good for the poor". Often, they try to convince communists that Marxian ideals would be better achieved using capitalist means; there is nothing wrong with the Marxian ideals, only the means are wrong. In other words, the challenge that they throw up is not adversarial but friendly in nature and, therefore, lacks conviction, bellicosity, and comprehensiveness to unnerve the Left. But when it comes to criticizing the RSS or the BJP, Indian liberals are extremely hostile and malicious; they are, in the words of Kristol, more anti-anti-communist than anti-communist.

To begin with, they mostly talk economics, seldom political economy. When discussing, say, the complicated issue of power sector reforms, experts mention the need of "political will". As if political will were just one of the (less important) prerequisites for power reforms, in the process completely ignoring practical aspects such as the willingness of politicians to carry out reforms, the incentives the politicians have to carry out reforms, the might of the vested interests, and the nature of political debate. The public discourse remains mired in Leftist catchwords and Gandhian sentimentalism. So, how do you intend to undertake something as gargantuan as power sector reforms? Nobody knows.

Former Prime Minister P. V. Narasimha Rao and his Finance Minister (later Prime Minister) Manmohan Singh are widely regarded as the authors of India's economic reforms. Yet, they never exhibited the courage of conviction to own up the revolution they had effected. Always diffident and defensive on the question of free market, they try to emphasize continuity with, rather than breach from, the Nehruvian past. I remember a lecture by Rao at

Delhi's India International Centre in the winter of 2000, in which he eulogized Nehru and the disastrous policies he followed in the first decades after Independence. Similarly, Singh spoke against privatization in 2003-04 when former Disinvestment Minister Arun Shourie stepped up the sell-off process.

Now, contrast this ideological diffidence and political timidity with Thatcher's conviction for liberalism. I quote at length from her memoirs, *The Downing Street Years*. She writes:

> I had grown up in a household that was neither poor nor rich. We had to economize each day in order to enjoy the occasional luxury. My father's background as a grocer is sometimes cited as the basis for my economic philosophy. So it was—and is—but his original philosophy encompassed more than simply ensuring that incomings showed a small surplus over outgoings at the end of the week. My father was both a practical man and a man of theory. He liked to connect the progress of our corner shop with the great complex romance of international trade which recruited people all over the world to ensure that a family in Grantham [Thatcher's hometown] could have on its table rice from India, coffee from Kenya, sugar from the West Indies and spices from five continents. Before I read a line from the great liberal economists, I knew from my father's accounts that the free market was like a vast sensitive nervous system, responding to events and signals all over the world to meet the ever-changing needs of peoples in different countries, from different classes, of different religions, with a kind of benign indifference to their status. Governments acted on a much smaller store of conscious information and, by contrast, were themselves "blind forces" blundering about in the dark, and obstructing the operations of markets rather than improving them. The economic history of Britain for the next forty years confirmed and amplified almost every item of my father's practical economics. In effect, I had been equipped at an early age with the ideal mental outlook and tools of analysis for reconstructing an economy ravaged by state socialism.

It is not my purpose to compare Thatcher with the likes of Rao and Manmohan Singh, for people of conviction can never be bracketed with the weathercocks. I rate Thatcher as one of the greatest leaders to have ruled in any part of the globe at any point of time. For her, liberalism in polity and economy was an article of faith and not a matter of expedience; and, being a woman of ideals, she made it a point to give a concrete shape to her political philosophy. On the other hand, Rao and Singh were at best technocrats, who had earlier implemented socialist policies in the same detached manner with which they carried out economic reforms.

Worse still, liberals argue as if liberalization were a necessary evil they have been forced to perpetrate upon a people who otherwise are contented with socialist policies (remember that despicable phrase "capitalism with a human face", which is based on the assumption that capitalism is essentially exploitative?). I will quote Bimal Jalan, former governor of the Reserve Bank of India and an eminent economist. He has held several administrative and advisory positions in the government of India, including those of finance secretary and chairman of the Economic Advisory Council to the Prime Minister. He has also represented India at the World Bank. In his book, *India's Economic Policy* (1996), he writes:

> Too often in India, a debate on economic policies becomes a debate on economic theory and ideology. Is liberalization theoretically superior to government intervention or is it not? Is globalization consistent with national sovereignty or is it not? Is reform of the public sector consistent with our socialist ideals or is it not? This is a sterile debate. The simple question that we should be focusing on is: what policies are needed to reduce inefficiency and waste in the allocation and use of our national resources? A more efficient and productive economy, which yields more output per unit of input, is good for the poor. It is good for national sovereignty and national security. It is, above all, consistent with a just and equitable society.

A "sterile debate"? Unfortunately, it seldom becomes a debate, sterile or otherwise; for, the champions of liberalization shy away from it, and the public discourse continues to be dominated by the Left. It is a vicious circle: reformers fear debate because they don't have the courage to face the influential Left; and the Left remains influential because economic reformers don't have the courage to challenge the Left.

Notice that Jalan has no ideological or theoretical problems with socialism; notice "our socialist ideals". The attitude of Jalan is guided by the logic of efficiency—"a more efficient and productive economy . . . is good for the poor": this is the logic of a manager rather than that of a reformer. For, unless a reformer takes the *ancien regime* head on ideologically, there is no hope for the success of reforms in the long run.

Let's see what Jalan has to say about privatization. The case of privatization, he says, "is not based on any presumed inherent superiority of private enterprises over public enterprises. Nor is it based on any ideological grounds." The truth is that the campaign for privatization has to be based on ideological grounds. Otherwise, it would be impossible to counter the Left's charge that public enterprises are "family silver", national property, crown jewels, etc. and that they are being "sold for a song". In fact, this was the reason that the government could not privatize a single state-run company of any consequence in the first nine years of economic reforms. It was only in early 2000 that the government could garner some courage to sell Modern Food Industries Ltd to Hindustan Lever Ltd. Such was the terror of the Leftist rhetoric, and the corresponding cravenness of liberalizers, that no government official ever mentioned the word "privatization" till 1998, when Finance Minister Yashwant Sinha uttered it in his Budget speech!

Like other votaries of economic reforms, Jalan unquestioningly accepts conventional wisdom and goes along with the socialist fiction that the public sector was the need of the hour after Independence. He writes:

> There was a time, soon after independence, when the public sector was regarded as the principal instrument for raising the level of savings and growth in the economy . . . the government, therefore, had to take upon itself the task of mobilizing the necessary

> financial and technical resources, and set up new industries in the public sector . . . .
>
> The government did succeed in mobilizing substantial resources through taxes and borrowings and pumping them into the public sector. A large number of enterprises . . . opened up many parts of the country which had seen no industrial activity in the past. India also became a sizeable producer of machinery, steel and heavy equipment in which the industrial world had a virtual monopoly. In these and other ways, the public sector began to symbolize the hopes and aspirations of a nation which had become free after a long political struggle.

Jalan seems to have unquestioningly accepted the unsubstantiated claim that the public sector at any point of time was the need of the hour; that, indeed, it was imperative to set up the public sector; that it was a historic necessity. In this context, I would quote from an excellent report, "So Many Lost Years: The Public Sector Before and After Reforms," prepared by Laveesh Bhandari and Omkar Goswami under the auspices of the National Council of Applied Economic Research (NCAER) in March 2000. According to this report:

> In making a case for state ownership, India's policy-makers ignored some basic facts . . . . By 1947 India' modern industrial or factory sector accounted for over 10 per cent of national income—a ratio that was well above any other de-colonized country with comparable per capita income. More than two-thirds of this factory sector output was due to the entrepreneurial drive of Indian capitalists, who set up a large cotton textile industry (accounting for 4% of GDP of a predominantly agrarian country), had a significant presence in coal mines, commissioned three iron and steel mills (Tata Iron & Steel in 1911, Indian Iron & Steel in the 1920s, and Visverswaraya Iron & Steel in the 1930s), and were involved in shipping and ship-building, cement plants, engineering units, sugar mills, glass factories, and many other industrial activities . . . . Indian entrepreneurs had [also] made

their presence felt in the jute industry which, until World War I, was a preserve of colonial firms.

India also had the necessary institutions for corporate growth: an efficient and well-knit railway system, relatively good ports, a large banking and insurance sector, and three very active, well-developed stock exchanges. Thus, by the early 1950s, India was the only de-colonized country that had the funds, the institutions, and the entrepreneurial base for large-scale private sector industrial development.

Further, "in 1950, India's per capita income was around $50. Yet, industrial output accounted for more than 20 % of its national income. In other words, despite mass poverty, by 1950 India had succeeded in creating an industrial base that was disproportionately larger than the trend."

Another important point raised by the NCAER report is: "Since almost all of industrial development was under the private sector, and over half of it was due to Indian entrepreneurship, there was no obvious dearth of private entrepreneurial ability in post-colonial India."

The purpose of quoting the NCAER report at length is just to underline the fact that the public sector never had a strong case. Either Jalan, despite his eminence as an economist, has completely internalized Leftist fiction on the origin of the public sector in India, or is unwilling to take on the might of the Leftist bombast when he says that "the public sector began to symbolize the hopes and aspirations of a nation which had become free after a long political struggle".

The idea is not to denigrate Jalan, but to show how Leftist influence has dominated his way of thinking—indeed, the liberal way of thinking. In fact, intellectual influence of the Left is visible not only in academics and the media but also in arts, culture, and literature. The received wisdom may have it that Red is dead, that the demolition of Berlin Wall and collapse of the Soviet Union has done away with the Leftist menace; socialists may be politically scattered and shattered; but their influence is still greatly disproportionate to their political strength. They may be too weak to capture power, but they are strong enough to wreak havoc with the making of policy, implementation of economic reforms, improving governance, and guarding against the enemy of the nation.

Unfortunately, the liberal is too prone to escape the trap of Leftist rhetoric. For instance, he passionately defends secularism—a futile exercise, as we shall see in the chapter on secularism. In general, the Indian intellectual, more or less, believes in this curious mixture of half-truths and lies, of negationist history and Marxist mythology. And this is the abyss from which the liberal can never come out. He fails to recognize the fact that liberty—which he cherishes as the ultimate ideal and value—cannot exist in abstraction. According to Hayek, "Paradoxical as it may appear, it is probably true that a successful free society will always in a large measure be a tradition-bound society." Now, for the Indian liberal anything "tradition-bound" is anathema; and if the tradition is Hindu in essence, as it is in the case of India—whatever the purveyors of "composite culture" may say—he can only revile it.

It may be argued that a tradition-bound society is not a necessary prerequisite for a successful free society, that liberty will thrive better in a society that is not under the dead hand of the past, that in fact tradition and a transcendent morality is antithetical to liberty—this is, more or less, the position of libertarians. In fact, it is the libertarian who carries forward the beacon of classical liberalism; the people for whom the term liberal is generally used are the ones who have actually subverted classical liberalism, as the *Dictionary of Philosophy* rightly pointed out. The libertarians in Europe and the US dread the increasing scope of collectivism and of government intervention in economy rather than of decreasing role of the community. Thinkers like Friedman and Ayn Rand can be categorized as libertarians.

The problem with the Aiyars and the Jalans is that they are not even libertarians. For the Western libertarians may not have great love for tradition, values, and community (which conservative thinkers like Edmund Burke, Mathew Arnold, Michael Oakshotte, Richard Weaver, and Jeffrey Hart exhibit), but they are very sure on some basic issues, the most important of them is their opposition to the Leftist rhetoric in all forms and in every area, whether it is economic, political, or cultural. And they are vehement in their criticism of the Left.

Indian liberals, however, are *nice* people. They read the right kind of authors (Edward Said and Noam Chomsky, for instance), and quote them adoringly; they pontificate over the fate of secularism and make the right kind of noises (the rise of communalism and fascism in India); they espouse cool causes (empowerment of dalits, uplift of women, awareness about AIDS, eradication of child labor, amelioration of the condition of slum-dwellers); they hang their heads in shame when Babri Masjid is demolished (and keep mum over the spread of Islamic terror). Nice People: they go into raptures over the plays by Vijay Tendulkar (or by any other hater of Hindu society); they are the connoisseurs of High Art and High Culture; they visit Kamani Auditorium and Vadhera Art Gallery; combine good etiquette with Left-libber rhetoric; they do not believe in offending anything chic, especially if it is as sacrosanct as received wisdom. Why think anything that has not been thought earlier? And why say anything that has not been said earlier? The veil of received wisdom is impenetrable, like *maya*, covering the reality. Which ensures that the Indian intellectual will never be "mugged by reality."

2 Tyranny of Decibels

In a country where sloganeering is confused with eloquence and platitudes with wisdom, it is hardly surprising that shouting passes off as the cry of the long-suffering, silent majority. Needless to say, nobody bothers to examine the authenticity of any cry: a cry, by virtue of being a cry, is always authentic. Or, so it is believed.

Intellectuals' favorite weapon is *argumentum ad hominem*—a fallacy in which the arguer rather than the argument is attacked. High decibels enhance the lethality of the weapon. So, now decibels perform the function what in saner times cogency of argument used to do. If you dare to challenge the tyranny of decibels, you will be, well, shouted down. The downtrodden are being neglected and pauperized in the liberalized economy, cry the self-proclaimed champions of the poor. If you dare to challenge this, or ask for any evidence to substantiate such an assertion, you would be immediately branded as a stooge of the World Bank, or a lackey of the diabolical multinational corporations (MNCs), or both. The Muslims are being "stereotyped" by the media and the West, shout the ultra-secular liberals. If you know a little bit of Islam and its inherently intolerant message, you are likely to point out that there is no "stereotyping", that Islam is, well, like that only, and that Islam is what Islam does (and it is not what the Mushirul Hasans and the Edward Saids say it is), you would be denounced as an ignorant bigot. Hindu society is most iniquitous, unjust, and unfair in the world, in which a small minority of upper castes oppress and exploit their less fortunate brethren, scream Leftist intellectuals and casteist leaders like Kanshi Ram, Lalu Prasad Yadav, and Mayawati. If you have the courage to challenge such canards, you are inarguably a status quoist, an apologist of the barbaric caste system, and of course a Hindu fundamentalist.

Interestingly, you will face only accusations and allegations; no reason or evidence is expected to substantiate the grave charges against you. You may ask for evidence to support the allegation that you are a stooge of the World Bank, you may point out that you have never visited any office of the infamous bank, but no—there is no reprieve. You may argue, they won't: they will shout, and you will be shouted down. Similarly, once the high priests of secular-liberal inquisition brand you as communal, fascist, or anti-poor, there is no way you can challenge that. There will not even be a mock trial; only the charge is read out and immediately it becomes the verdict; your views will not even be heard; if you insist, you will be, well, shouted down. The progeny of Ambedkar and Mandal are no less vociferous; if you challenge the wisdom of affirmative action and caste-based politics, they will see to it that your arguments are drowned in a deluge of allegations. Abuse is the argument.

A number of factors—political, social, and cultural—sustain and nurture the tyranny of decibels. An important factor is the pusillanimity and dishonesty of the political class. It works in the following fashion: The government decides to liberalize, say, the labor sector. This would entail some changes in the archaic labor laws, arguably the worst legacy of the socialist era. There is a howl of protest from the communist parties, trade union leaders, and Leftwing intellectuals. The accusations are on expected lines: the government is under the evil influence of global capitalism; politicians are the lackeys of big industry; the proposed labor reforms are against workers and the nation. The Opposition will join in the fun; decibels will grow with time.

The result? The government would start thinking, rethinking, re-rethinking: are the reforms so bad? Doubts, misgivings, apprehensions will start bothering senior ministers: will labor reforms cost us votes? The casualties would be reason and common sense. Nobody in the political class has the courage to face up to basic facts. To begin with, not many people would be affected—adversely or otherwise—by labor reforms, for organized labor is less than 8 per cent of India's work force. So, even if one assumes that the entire labor force would be at the mercy of employers after reforms—a ludicrous assumption though it is—more than 92 per cent of the work force will benefit in the bargain, as flexible labor laws attract more investment and create jobs. Secondly, the protesters are the very people responsible for many of ills of the economy; and they are against change because this will marginalize them. But few ministers are willing to recognize this fact. Nor do they realize that the self-styled champions of labor are actually representatives of a very small, and privileged, part of the work force—organized labor. Neither politically nor morally is it justified to continue with the outdated labor laws. But the political class is too pusillanimous and intellectually bankrupt to see reason, common sense, and fairness, all of which are lost in the cacophony of banality.

Let's take another example, that of privatization. Family silver is being sold for a song to pay the grocer's bill, cry the Leftwing intellectual and the Rightwing ideologue in an unusual unison. To which, former Disinvestment Minister Arun Shourie retorts: public sector undertakings (PSUs) are not family silver but bleeding ulcers, a constant drain on the public exchequer. Despite documented evidence to support Shourie's position, the howls of protest do not die down. In the 1990s, for instance, the government had to pump in about Rs. 60,000 crore in central PSUs alone, whereas it received around Rs. 20,000 crore from this family silver. Similarly, between 1988-89 and 1997-98, PSUs in the non-monopoly sector recorded losses in every financial year save one, the total losses being about Rs. 1,900 crore. Report after CAG report has pointed out the inefficiencies and wastefulness of PSUs; the CAG has on more than one occasion commented that the profits of PSUs are essentially because of the monopoly in certain sectors. The Public Enterprise Surveys have also brought out a similar picture. In the survey for 2002-03, the total profits excluding that of petroleum, power, and coal—the sectors where PSUs enjoy market dominance—were a little more than Rs. 1,000 crore. The total investment on PSUs runs in lakhs of crores.

Yet, PSUs are "national property" which should not be handed to private hands. Nobody is willing to see in which fashion the "nation" controls these companies; nobody recognizes the simple fact that "nation"—as far as control over such family silver is concerned—means a Satish Sharma or Ram Naik, a Pramod Mahajan or a Laloo Prasad Yadav; nobody realizes that it is impossible to run PSUs on commercial lines when there are myriad pressures of political compulsions and vested interests. Yet, the protests continue, and the politician continues to tremble at their raucousness.

The tyranny of decibels is also supported by social and cultural factors. One is rampant philistinism. Reading habits of Indians are pathetic; people are simply not interested in reading anything once they have acquired their degrees. This helps professional revolutionaries; they are free to spread their canards and disinformation. Worse still, the so-called Rightwing, namely, the Sangh Parivar, just echoes the views of the Left on a variety of issues, particular the economic matters. Whether it is privatization or foreign investment, labor reforms or opening up of the farm sector, there is an uncanny similarity in the views of the Left and the supposedly Right.

When decibels rule the roost, it is not surprising that the shrillest and the loudest noisemakers appear to be the most convincing campaigners; fashionable radicals and often vested interests masquerade as the crusaders of the truth. One reason for the unchallenged regime of decibels is that the noisemakers always use fashionable causes—peace, communal harmony, education for slum children, clean environment, poverty alleviation; long runs the list. Now, usually decent people don't challenge the objectives of various noisemakers—which is unexceptionable, since nobody in their right minds would say that war is good, or that environment should not be cleaned up. But the problem arises that they also tend to acquiesce in, or ignore, the means recommended to achieve these objectives. And since Leftists and Left-libbers monopolize all the fashionable causes, the means also belong to the socialist inventory, leading to the most unpleasant consequences. Poverty alleviation results in a huge drain on the public exchequer, which in turn leads to higher taxes with the cascading ill effects on the entire economy. When he was in the Opposition, Finance Minister P. Chidambaram wrote in an article that as much as about Rs. 1,50,000 crore were spent per annum at the turn of the century, with little benefit going to the poor (It is another matter that, like a typical liberal, he brazenly and abjectly accepted the diktats of the Left when he later joined the Manmohan Singh government). In fact, the resultant adverse effects on the economy more than nullify whatever little good the poor derive from the poverty alleviation schemes, for without these schemes there would be much more economic activity, resulting in more jobs and better social security. Similarly, the suggested means to attain peace are nothing but an abject surrender to Pakistan. Communal harmony is just another way of bashing not merely the BJP, the Sangh Parivar, but often the entire Hindu society. The Left sets the agenda and the tune; intellectuals, because of their mental lethargy, are unable to see through the game and form the chorus. In fact, it is the intellectuals who play the most important role in sustaining the tyranny of decibels. They continue with the chorus even when the Left is not playing its orchestra.

The intellectual bankruptcy of the so-called Indian Right just aggravates the matter. For, instead of effectively countering the Left's hidden agenda, the semi-educated knickerwallahs either capitulate or lapse into gibberish. On economic issues, they just echo the political philosophy of the Left, which is nothing but ideological surrender; on the other issues, they talk incoherently in a dialect that is almost incomprehensible. Not surprisingly, the Left gets a free hand to set the agenda and conduct the public discourse as per its own caprices and fads. Having lost the battle for minds, the Right starts finding scapegoats—English newspapers, the "progeny of Macaulay and Marx", multinational corporations, the World Bank, the US. The Right also imitates Leftist tactics: shout at and, if possible, shout down the opponent. Needless to say, the effect of such developments on public discourse could not be more deleterious.

With a public discourse already distorted beyond recognition, and the motto of "high living and no thinking" gaining ground, the tyranny of decibels will feel no threat to its regime. The shrillest voices will continue to be considered the most eloquent and cogent.

3 Arundhati Roy
Sentimentalism Oozing from Every Pore

If you want to know what chic is, just have a look at Arundhati Roy's recent writings. The latest intellectual fads, fashionable phraseology, high-sounding rhetoric, sexy philanthropy, magnificent gibberish, high humbug—you will find everything there. It all adds up to great style, but with little substance.

Nietzsche once wrote, "I want to say in ten sentences what others say in ten volumes—and what they do *not* say." In this respect, Roy is the antithesis of Nietzsche: her sentimentalism drives her to write rambling, long-winded essays on almost everything under the sun—from nuclear bombs to hydroelectric projects, from the pathos of tribals to the alleged perspicacity of Chomsky; write, without the necessary wherewithal, without the backing of any scholarship, without even proper understanding of any of the subjects. Borrowing heavily from Leftist clichés and trendy shibboleths, adding a bit of Gandhi-like love-for-pristine-things, and embellishing her arguments with a liberal dose of anti-Americanism and anti-capitalism, she produces essays which *Outlook* magazine—that platform for political correctness and cretinism—loves to publish. And since she has been acknowledged in the West, as a winner of Booker Prize, her verbose denunciations pass off as eloquence, and half-baked analysis as expertise.

After winning the Booker, she entered the arena of public discourse with a bang—even literally. She wrote "The End of Imagination" for the August 3, 1998, issue of *Outlook* in which she fumed against the nuclear explosion carried out in May 1998 by the newly-elected Atal Bihari Vajpayee government. She wrote:

> There's nothing new or original left to be said about nuclear weapons. There can be nothing more humiliating for a writer of fiction to have to do than restate a case that has, over the years, already been made by other people in other parts of the world, and made passionately, eloquently and knowledgeably.
>
> I am prepared to grovel. To humiliate myself abjectly, because, in the circumstances, silence would be indefensible. So those of you who are willing: let's pick our parts, put on these discarded costumes and speak our second-hand lines in this sad second-hand play. But let's not forget that the stakes we're playing for are huge. Our fatigue and our shame could mean the end of us. The end of our children and our children's children. Of everything we love. We have to reach within ourselves and find the strength to think. To fight.

She began honestly, admitting that nothing original should be expected of her: what followed was an almost 7,800-word account of how the world would come to an end! (I wonder how many million words she would produce if she had anything "new or original" to say). She wrote:

> If there is a nuclear war, our foes will not be China or America or even each other. Our foe will be the earth herself. The very elements—the sky, the air, the land, the wind and water—will all turn against us. Their wrath will be terrible.
>
> Our cities and forests, our fields and villages will burn for days. Rivers will turn to poison. The air will become fire. The wind will spread the flames. When everything there is to burn has burned and the fires die, smoke will rise and shut out the sun. The earth will be enveloped in darkness. There will be no day. Only interminable night . . . .

Terrible future. Actually, the nuclear bomb can wreak a great deal of havoc even without a war:

> Not only can the Government use it [the bomb] to threaten the Enemy, they can use it to declare war on their own people. Us.
>
> In 1975, one year after India first dipped her toe into the nuclear sea, Mrs. Gandhi declared the Emergency. What will 1999 bring? There's talk of cells being set up to monitor anti-national activity. Talk of amending cable laws to ban networks "harming national culture" (*The Indian Express*, July 3). Of churches being struck off the list of religious places because "wine is served" (announced and retracted, *The Indian Express*, July 3, *The Times of India*, July 4). Artists, writers, actors, and singers are being harassed, threatened (and succumbing to the threats). Not just by goon squads, but by instruments of the government. And in courts of law . . .

All this because we have nuclear tests! A number of political analysts have written on the reasons that compelled Indira Gandhi to declare Emergency; but none of them have come up with an explanation as fantastic as Roy's: Pokhran I caused Emergency. At the time of writing these lines, more than eight years have elapsed since Pokhran II; yet, unfortunately for the liberal Nostradamus, Ms Roy, the country has not witnessed another spell of dictatorship.

Now, it is another matter that she might see in the activities of the lunatic fringe of the Sangh Parivar an undeclared dictatorship. But such activities were there even before the BJP-led government assumed office or when India crossed the nuclear Rubicon. In fact, there is no cause-and-effect relationship between possessing a nuclear bomb and being a dictatorship. The US, the UK, and France are nuclear but they are democracies (though Roy does not believe they are, especially the US, as we shall see later). In her analysis, causality is the first casualty. But Roy does not pause to ponder over the any causality or casualty, or the lack of it, she alludes to;

she moves on to the maze of development economics. According to her:

> We are a nation of nearly a billion people. In development terms we rank No. 138 out of the 175 countries listed in the UNDP's Human Development Index. More than 400 million of our people are illiterate and live in absolute poverty, over 600 million lack even basic sanitation and over 200 million have no safe drinking water.

It is true that in terms of human development India is a laggard; but this is not linked with the expenditure incurred on nuclear tests or with defence expenditure. It is infantile to assume that India would have made dramatic progress in human development had there been no nuclear tests. In the aftermath of the Cold War, there was considerable decline in defence expenditures in many important countries, but this did not cause any great increase in human development in the concerned countries; there was no "peace dividend", as hoped for by peaceniks.

Before you could make any sense of the grandiloquent baloney she is uttering without any stop, she has moved on to the rarefied realms of Indology and political philosophy:

> Whether or not there has ever been a single civilization that could call itself "Indian Civilization", whether or not India was, is, or ever will become a cohesive cultural entity, depends on whether you dwell on the differences or the similarities in the cultures of the people who have inhabited the subcontinent for centuries. India, as a modern nation state, was marked out with precise geographical boundaries, in their precise geographical way, by a British Act of Parliament in 1899. Our country, as we know it, was forged on the anvil of the British Empire for the entirely unsentimental reasons of commerce and administration. But even as she was born, she began her struggle against her creators. So is India Indian? It's a tough question. Let's just say that we're an ancient people learning to live in a recent nation.

What is true is that India is an artificial State—a State that was created by a government, not a people. A State created from the top down, not the bottom up. The majority of India's citizens will not (to this day) be able to identify her boundaries on a map, or say which language is spoken where or which god is worshipped in what region. Most are too poor and too uneducated to have even an elementary idea of the extent and complexity of their own country. The impoverished, illiterate agrarian majority have no stake in the State. And indeed, why should they, how can they, when they don't even know what the State is? To them, India is, at best, a noisy slogan that comes around during the elections. Or a montage of people on Government TV programmes wearing regional costumes and saying *Mera Bharat Mahan*.

So, India does not exist. At any rate, not as a nation, not as a civilization; merely an administrative convenience, and that too of the erstwhile colonial masters. This is in tune with the official philosophy of British imperialists that India was merely a "geographical expression"—a thought not much different from that of communists. If India never existed, where did Columbus want to reach? Why is the arrival of Vasco de Gama at Calicut considered a major event of world history? What did Megasthenes refer to by his treatise *Indica*? Why did Shankaracharya set up four seats of learning in four different parts of the country, and not merely his native Kerala? Why did every Hindu king want to become a Chakravarti Samrat, ruling the entire nation (even though few succeeded in it)? And why did even Muslim kings of north India want to reach the natural boundaries of the Himalayas, the Arabian Sea, and the Bay of Bengal? Why did AL Basham write his monumental, *The Wonder That Was India*?

Arundhati Roy does not like to answer any of these questions. In any case, she is in a hurry. Quickly paying her homage to Mahatma Gandhi (a necessary ritual these days, as he is very popular among the Left and cool intellectuals), she makes a whirlwind visit to Babri Masjid and says all the good things about communal harmony, etc. And then she moves to the grand finale:

> Who the hell is the Prime Minister to decide whose finger will be on the nuclear button that could turn everything we love—our

> earth, our skies, our mountains, our plains, our rivers, our cities and villages—to ash in an instant? Who the hell is he to reassure us that there will be no accidents? How does he know? Why should we trust him? What has he ever done to make us trust him? What have any of them ever done to make us trust them?
>
> The nuclear bomb is the most anti-democratic, anti-national, anti-human, outright evil thing that man has ever made.
>
> If you are religious, then remember that this bomb is Man's challenge to God.
>
> It's worded quite simply: We have the power to destroy everything that You have created.
>
> If you're not (religious), then look at it this way. This world of ours is four thousand, six hundred million years old.
>
> It could end in an afternoon.

Quite apart from the impertinent language ("Who the hell is the Prime Minister"), the outburst is so puerile that nobody would have noticed it had it not come from the pen of a Booker winner. The Prime Minister is the lawfully elected chief executive of the largest democracy in the world. Trust him or don't trust him, he remains the leader because the country has elected him to rule.

When it is not puerility, it is excessive sentimentalism:

> If protesting against having a nuclear bomb implanted in my brain is anti-Hindu and anti-national, then I secede. I hereby declare myself an independent, mobile republic. I am a citizen of the earth. I own no territory. I have no flag. I'm female, but have nothing against eunuchs. My policies are simple. I'm willing to sign any nuclear non-proliferation treaty or nuclear test ban treaty that's going. Immigrants are welcome. You can help me design our flag.

And all along we thought that it is subnational territories that seek secession! But here is the megalomania of an individual that is seeking secession! We are already aware of a "mobile republic"—Osama bin Laden. He has also seceded from civilization; and he is waging a war against civilization. Arundhati Roy is not a

terrorist, but she is definitely an anarchist; she does not know what is good, but she knows what is bad: whatever exists is bad; the entire world—human civilization, as it exists—is bad, unjust, iniquitous. She does not know what this world should be replaced with; but she knows that it should be replaced. Replaced, perhaps, by a New World.

But haven't we heard all this before? Hitler wanted to create a New World, so did Stalin, and Mao, and Pol Pot. And what did we get? Gas chambers, slave camps, mass murder; killings on a scale mankind had not known earlier. She is obviously oblivious of the fact that any negation of the world, anarchist or otherwise, is the surest recipe for disaster.

From her political philosophy, we move on to her economics. Her understanding of economics is as sentimental as is her political philosophy. In an essay, "Power Politics: Comeback of Rumpelstiltskin?" in *Outlook* (November 27, 2000), she writes:

> Let's begin at the beginning. What does privatization *really* mean? Essentially, it is the transfer of public productive assets from the State to private companies. Productive assets include natural resources. Earth, forest, water, air. These are assets that the State holds in trust for the people it represents. In a country like India, 70 per cent of the population lives in rural areas. That's 700 million people. Their lives depend directly on access to natural resources. To snatch these away and sell them as stock to private companies is a process of barbaric dispossession on a scale that has no parallel in history.
>
> What happens when you "privatize" something as essential to human survival as water? What happens when you commodify water and say that only those who can come up with the cash to pay the "market price" can have it? In 1999, the government of Bolivia privatized the public water supply system in the city of Cochacomba, and signed a 40-year lease with Bechtel, a giant US engineering firm. The first thing Bechtel did was to triple the price of water. Hundreds of thousands of people simply couldn't afford it any more. Citizens came out on the streets to protest. A transport strike brought the entire city to a standstill. Hugo Ban-

> zer, the former Bolivian dictator (now the President) ordered the police to fire at the crowds. Six people were killed, 175 injured and two children blinded. The protest continued because people had no options—what's the option to thirst? In April 2000, Banzer declared Martial Law. The protest continued. Eventually Bechtel was forced to flee its offices. Now it's trying to extort a $12-million exit payment from the Bolivian government.

So, privatization in India means "a process of barbaric dispossession on a scale that has no parallel in history", as 70 per cent of the population lives in villages and is directly dependent on "natural resources". As a correspondent of *The Financial Express*, I have covered privatization as a beat since privatization really started. And I have come across a variety of arguments against it, but few so bizarre; only uneducated kind of people can argue in such a fashion. Uneducated, because there is hardly any public sector undertaking (PSU) that is engaged in agriculture; in other words, the rural areas have little to do with PSUs. The public sector and privatization are primarily urban issues; I don't remember any of the leaders of farmers, from Mahindra Singh Tikait to Sharad Joshi, saying anything about privatization; it is not their concern.

Her knowledge base on the public sector and privatization is really narrow. Otherwise, she would not have written:

> The Indian public sector company, Bharat Heavy Electricals Ltd (Bhel), manufactured and even exported world-class power equipment. All that's changed now. Over the years, our own government has starved it of orders, cut off funds for research and development and more or less edged it out of a dignified existence. Today Bhel is no more than a sweatshop. It is being forced into "joint ventures" (one with GE and one with Siemens) where its only role is to provide cheap, unskilled labor while they provide the equipment and the technology.

To set the record straight, Bhel is not a "sweatshop"; it can boast of a highly skilled workforce. An efficiently run service-sector PSU, Bhel has thrived in the post-liberalization era. As per

the unaudited results for the quarter ended December 31, 2005, Bhel posted a net profit of Rs. 423.19 crore as compared to Rs. 237.4 crore for the quarter ended December 31, 2004. In the same quarter, total income (net of excise) stood at Rs. 3,445.45 crore, up from Rs. 2,386.47 crore in the corresponding quarter previous financial year. It is for this reason that MNCs like Siemens and GE want to tie up with Bhel—and there is no great conspiracy involved in such arrangements. Nor such arrangements have anything to do with privatization.

Essentially, privatization means the rollback of the state; the state makes a bow, so that the entrepreneurial spirits of society could do properly what the state is unable to do efficiently: privatization is the most visible and poignant feature of the transition from socialism to capitalism. Now, let's extend Roy's who-the-hell-is-the-prime-minister argument. Do the prime minister, his ministers, and the myriad bureaucrats know how to hold "earth, forest, water, air" which are, in her words, the "assets that the State holds in trust for the people it represents"? Roy has herself written reams and reams about the incompetence and corruption of the government, the system, etc; so why is she opposed to a loosening of the state's hold over natural assets?

Shorn of all rhetoric, her stance is clearly that of the Leftists *when not in power*: she is opposed to a state that is politically powerful; yet, she wants it to be economically powerful, so she favors a state to "hold" all the natural assets. All communist parties in India railed against Pokhran II; but they celebrated when the Stalinist Russia and Moaist China went nuclear.

Roy's examples are also typically Leftist: citing exceptions as the rule. She cites one instance of failed privatization in a town nobody knew existed, Cochacomba; she refuses to see the wonders done by Margaret Thatcher in Great Britain, how privatization played a key role in the revival of the British economy which had become a basket case before the Thatcherite revolution, how this inspired countries all over the world to follow suit, including communist China (and the Left Front government of West Bengal, which is also privatizing state PSUs). It is like asking the police

force to be dismantled because one cop was involved in some robbery on the ground that if cops and robbers do the same thing, why do you need a police department!

Privatization irks Arundhati Roy because she can't stand the market economy or capitalism. This becomes evident from her reverence for Noam Chomsky, a professional rebel from the US. He is a favorite of India's liberals and Leftists. Roy writes in another essay, "The Loneliness of Noam Chomsky" (*Outlook*, September 2, 2003):

> Today, thanks to Noam Chomsky and his fellow media analysts, it is almost axiomatic for thousands, possibly millions, of us that public opinion in "free market" democracies is manufactured just like any other mass market product—soap, switches, or sliced bread. We know that while, legally and constitutionally, speech may be free, the space in which that freedom can be exercised has been snatched from us and auctioned to the highest bidders. Neoliberal capitalism isn,t just about the accumulation of capital (for some). It's also about the accumulation of power (for some), the accumulation of freedom (for some). Conversely, for the rest of the world, the people who are excluded from neoliberalism's governing body, it's about the *erosion* of capital, the *erosion* of power, the *erosion* of freedom. In the "free" market, free speech has become a commodity like everything else—justice, human rights, drinking water, clean air. It's available only to those who can afford it. And naturally, those who can afford it use free speech to manufacture the kind of product, confect the kind of public opinion, that best suits their purpose. (News they can use.) Exactly how they do this has been the subject of much of Noam Chomsky's political writing.

Notice "free market", where "justice, human rights" are mere commodities, "available only to those who can afford" them. But why are such commodities not available in Castro's Cuba, communist China, and theocratic Saudi Arabia? And why were they not available in the erstwhile Soviet Union? Chomsky *lives* in the US, and writes against the US government; Roy *lives* in India, and writes against the Indian government. How many Noam Chom-

skys and Arundhati Roys have written against the system in non-capitalist societies and *lived*?

As Nobel laureate Milton Friedman wrote in his magnum opus, *Capitalism and Freedom*, "Economic arrangements play a dual role in the promotion of a free society. On the one hand, freedom in economic arrangements is itself a component of freedom broadly understood, so economic freedom is an end in itself. In the second place, economic freedom is also an indispensable means towards the achievement of political freedom."

Further, "the kind of economic organization that provides economic freedom directly, namely, competitive capitalism, also promotes political freedom because it separates economic power from political power and in this way enables the one to offset the other."

Ayn Rand, another major political thinker of the twentieth century, is even more emphatic. She writes, "Is man free? In mankind's history, capitalism is the only system that answers: Yes."

According to Rand, "Capitalism is the only social system based on the recognition of individual rights, including property rights, in which all property is privately owned."

Since time immemorial, the basic motive of any economic activity has been profit or pecuniary reward. So, the most common definition of capitalism—as a system in which making profit is the motive of economic activity—is tautological. Capitalism is something more than that; it is the only system in which all the natural, inalienable rights of man—about which great liberal philosophers like Locke and Mill have written so extensively—get crystallized. And the right to property is the most important of these rights, for this right drills huge holes in the ramparts of the erstwhile all-powerful state. In the twentieth century, collectivists of various hues were able to fill up these holes; some of the consequences were Nazi Germany, Stalinist Russia, Moaist China, and Nehruvian India. Fortunately, the world has recognized the evilness of collectivism, and it is moving towards capitalism.

Arundhati Roy does not like that. Like a Leftist who refuses to believe in the goodness of capitalism, Roy deliberately shuts her

eyes. She is like Gandhari of *Mahabharat*: her blindness is self-imposed; because her lord and master, Dhritrashtra, is blind, she remains blindfolded all her life. Dhritrashtra's blindness is by compulsion, Gandhari's by choice; the Leftist's blindness is because of his ideology, Roy's—like Gandhari's—because she is slavishly following a blind master.

Otherwise, Roy would know that there is a direct correlation between capitalism and prosperity, between free market and responsible, responsive government, between economic freedom and political rights. It is not by accident that the most prosperous nations are the ones that follow the capitalist path. Not surprisingly, capitalism is the chosen path of almost all nations, from the erstwhile socialist India to the still (nominally) communist China. So, either there is some inherent virtue in capitalism, or there is some conspiracy of cosmic proportions which is cajoling or forcing nations all over the world to adopt the free market path. Roy seems to suspect some conspiracy.

However, conspiracies also happen at smaller, local levels. Take India, for instance. What we call progress or development is a fiction agreed upon; in actual fact, there is only ruthless exploitation. Roy cites her favorite cause: dams.

> A huge percentage of the displaced are tribal people (57.6 per cent in the case of the Sardar Sarovar Dam). Include Dalits and the figure becomes obscene. According to the Commissioner for Scheduled Castes and Tribes it's about 60 per cent. If you consider that tribal people account for only eight per cent, and Dalits 15 per cent, of India's population, it opens up a whole other dimension to the story. The ethnic "otherness" of their victims takes some of the pressure off the Nation Builders. It's like having an expense account. Someone else pays the bills. People from another country. Another world. India's poorest people are subsidizing the life-styles of her richest.

So, you see, the same old story: the rich exploit the poor! In fact, something worse than that: the "poorest people" subsidize "the lifestyles" of the "richest"! In other words, all the dalits and

tribals are poor, or "the poorest people," the ethnic others; and all the rest are the rich, or the richest, affording "life-styles." This is unquestioning acquiescence to V.P. Singh's theory that India is a "coalition" of warring castes and communities, the theory which emboldened him to implement the diabolical and divisive Mandal Commission report in 1990. A detailed analysis of this report is beyond the scope of this book. In a nutshell, one can say that the report is based on wrong premises and inadequate scholarship. For instance, the report denounces Hindu society as unique in iniquitousness, rigidity, and malevolence: "If religion was ever used as an opium of the masses, it was done in India." As if in the rest of the world was an egalitarian paradise! Further, the report mischievously used the alleged historical atrocities of one social group, the dalits, to justify the extension of reservation benefits for other backward castes like Yadavs and Kurmis (who never suffered such dalit-like discrimination). The Mandal Commission report was criticized even by many liberals as divisive and irrational; but Arundhati Roy accepts its logic without deliberating upon the assumptions and postulates it is based on, or upon the deplorable consequences it leads to. Worse still, she has added her literary sentimentalism to a crass political document that has done incalculable damage to Indian politics:

> The millions of displaced people don't exist anymore. When history is written they won't be in it. Not even as statistics. Some of them have subsequently been displaced three and four times—a dam, an artillery proof range, another dam, a uranium mine, a power project. Once they start rolling there's no resting place. The great majority is eventually absorbed into slums on the periphery of our great cities, where it coalesces into an immense pool of cheap construction labor (that builds more projects that displace more people). True, they're not being annihilated or taken to gas chambers, but I can warrant that the quality of their accommodation is worse than in any concentration camp of the Third Reich. They're not captive, but they redefine the meaning of liberty.

> And still the nightmare doesn't end. They continue to be uprooted even from their hellish hovels by government bulldozers that fan out on clean-up missions whenever elections are comfortingly far away and the urban rich get twitchy about hygiene. In cities like Delhi, they run the risk of being shot by the police for shitting in public places—like three slum-dwellers were, not more than two years ago.

Worse than the Third Reich? Now, either Roy is ignorant or she is indulging in dangerous hyperbole. Ours is definitely not the Third Reich, the biggest evidence of which is the fact that she published all her essays under review in India during a regime preponderated by a supposedly fascist group.

The problem with intellectuals like Arundhati Roy is that they are too lazy to use common sense, or even just look around, before coming to any conclusions. Slothfully, they reach out for the available Leftist explanations and slogans; the explanations are unquestioningly accepted and slogans religiously chanted. Otherwise, Roy would have seen that slum-dwellers, for whom her heart bleeds, are not as helpless creatures as she is hard-bent on showing. For, most of the time, they are not the victims but beneficiaries of the system: they encroach on (usually) government land; they use amenities such as water and electricity for free; they defecate in the open and dirty the environment, even though many of them can afford toilets—if they can afford color televisions, they can also afford toilets. Further, if and when they are evicted from their habitation, they are given alternative plots; in the case of Delhi, half of them sell off their plots and come back to slums. And it is not just the urban rich who "get twitchy about hygiene"; the middle and lower middle classes also find slums to be a nuisance.

In any case, the problems faced by dalits and tribals are because of the malady rather than bias in the system; for there are any number of cases in which members of upper castes have been subjected to similar apathy and callousness. But Roy is not willing to undertake a detailed scrutiny of the system, which might have opened her eyes to the havoc wrought by socialism since Inde-

pendence. Quite the contrary, she continues to borrow from the very people, the Leftists, whose ideas have all but ruined the nation. Every time she writes her verbose, often garrulous, essays in *Outlook*, she exposes herself as one who has suffered "the end of imagination".

4 Jawaharlal Nehru
Tryst with Socialism

The genesis of most political and economic problems India faces today can be traced to Jawaharlal Nehru. And he was the quintessential intellectual.

This is not to say that he was a bad man. In fact, Nehru can justly be called a good man: he was a scholar with varied interests and wide sympathies; he was an accomplished writer; as a politician, he was neither tyrannical nor venal—traits so common among successful leaders in Third World countries in the second half of the twentieth century. He was an intellectual who succeeded in politics. That was his biggest problem. It also became the nation's biggest problem.

As described in the opening chapter, an intellectual is a person who downplays the importance of empirical evidence and wants to change the world relying solely, or primarily, on intellect. And, as Sartre said, there cannot be an intellectual "without his being Leftwing". Nehru certainly was Leftwing, as is evident from his various writings and the policies that he imposed on the nation as its first Prime Minister.

In his article, "Swaraj and Socialism" (1928), he wrote: "Capitalism necessarily leads to exploitation of one man by another, one group by another, and one country by another. If, therefore, we are opposed to this [British] imperialism and exploitation, we must

also be opposed to capitalism. The only alternative that is offered to us is some form of socialism."

Nothing could be farther from the truth. For, as authors like Ayn Rand have pointed out, capitalism is the *only* system known to mankind that is free of exploitation. Socialism, on the other hand, leads to subjugation of individual life and liberty to the state. Unfortunately, communists have been quite successful in selling their lie that "capitalism necessarily leads to exploitation". Communists succeeded because they relentlessly indulged in guilt-mongering and by making argument with abuse (See the chapters Guilt: Weapon of Mass Deception and Tyranny of Decibels). Few thinkers and writers have garnered the courage to expose the lie; intellectuals have generally peddled this lie; Nehru too was among the purveyors of the communist lie.

The fact is that there is *no exploitation* in capitalism. It is the only system in which people—industrialists and workers, employers and employees, farmers and commodity traders—are free to buy and sell their services and goods at prices that are (objectively) determined by the market. In no other system do human beings enjoy such freedom: in feudalism the huge masses of people are treated as chattel by a handful of land-owning lords; communism ends up killing millions of people in the name of setting up a proletarian paradise and glorifying thugs like Stalin and Mao; fascism created Auschwitz and Dachau. Market economy, on the hand, offers freedom and prosperity. According to Rand, "Capitalism has created the highest standard of living ever known on earth. The evidence is incontrovertible. The contrast between West and East Berlin is the latest demonstration, like a laboratory experiment for all to see. Yet those who are loudest in proclaiming their desire to eliminate poverty are loudest in denouncing capitalism. Man's well-being is not their goal."

Obviously, Rand wrote this before the fall of the Berlin Wall and the re-unification of Germany into a market economy. Of course, in capitalism there are people who do very well and there are people who barely manage to survive. Indeed, there are huge disparities between wealth and income. But these are the com-

plexities of human existence. God or nature has not been egalitarian in distributing His or its bounties on mankind: some of us are good-looking, others are not; some of us are intelligent and bright, others are not; many of us are diligent, whereas others have little capacity for work; some of us enjoy a long, healthy life without taking good care of our bodies, whereas other people get afflicted with diseases for no fault of theirs; and long goes the list of good and bad qualities that seem to have been unevenly distributed among men and women. Most of us accept such arbitrariness as a given in life, as *fait accompli*. But when it comes to the distribution of wealth and income in capitalist society, we are unable—or unwilling—to accept inequality as a given. And among us, intellectuals find it extremely difficult to accept that capitalism is the natural system, which truly reflects the vicissitudes of life in its entirety. They look for alternatives, a search which takes them to the deserts of intellectualism; they end up chasing one mirage or the other; usually the mirage of socialism fascinates them. Nehru was no different. He also sought and found refuge in socialism. Hence his conviction, "The only alternative that is offered to us is some form of socialism."

Then, too, intellectuals suffer from the arrogance of believing that they can improve every thing around them. Thus, "the existing order" irritated Nehru; he was interested in "the great building-up of a socialized society". For this grand purpose, "the major obstructions have thus to be removed." He was against the "present economic system" because he felt it was causing the "destruction [of] vast numbers of human beings."

He got it all wrong. It was not capitalism that was leading to the destruction of men and societies when he wrote these lines in 1936. Two major events, the First World War (1914-18) and the economic depression a decade later, were largely responsible for the downslide in economy and living conditions at that time. As far as India and other colonies were concerned, it was, in fact, the absence of capitalism, and not its presence, that was responsible for their dismal economic and social conditions.

But Nehru's problem was that he, like other intellectuals, had blindly accepted the Leninist dogma—that imperialism was the final stage of capitalism and thus the culprit which needed to be thrown out root and branch was capitalism. In fact, it was not just socialist economy that enchanted Nehru; he accepted the entire socialist ideology hook, line, and sinker. In his presidential address to the Indian National Congress in Lucknow on April 12, 1936, he said:

> I am convinced that the only key to the solution of the world's problem and of India's problem lies in socialism, and when I use this word I do not do so in a vague humanitarian way but in the scientific economic sense. Socialism is, however, something even more than an economic doctrine; it is a *philosophy of life* and as such also it appeals to me. I see no way of ending the poverty, the vast unemployment, the degradation and subjection of the Indian people except through socialism. This involves vast and revolutionary changes in our political and social structure, the ending of vested interests in land and industry, as well as the feudal and autocratic Indian states system. This means the *ending of private property*, except in a restricted sense, and the replacement of the present profit system by a higher ideal of co-operative service. In short, it means a new civilization, radically different from the present capitalist order. Some glimpse we can have of this new civilization in the territories of the USSR . . . *If the future is full of hope it is largely because of Soviet Russia* and what it has done, and I am convinced that, if some world catastrophe does not intervene, this new civilization will spread to other lands and put an end to the wars and conflicts which capitalism feeds on. (emphasis added)

I wonder how Mahatma Gandhi and the supposedly Rightwing Congress leaders like Sardar Patel and Gobind Vallabh Pant allowed such loose talk—ending of private property, revolutionary changes in politics and society—at a gathering of the most important political party of the time, and let it pass without rebuttal. What is interesting is that such pompous homilies came at a time

when Stalin, in his endeavor to introduce "vast and revolutionary changes" in the Soviet Union, had already murdered his own millions of peasants and people. Collectivization of agriculture proved to be catastrophic not only for farmers but all of Russia. Even an apologist for the Left, Nobel Laureate Amartya Sen, has been forced to admit the reality of man-made famines in Stalinist Russia.

Objective observers and researchers have presented a much more horrific picture of Stalinist Russia. Anne Applebaum is one such scholar who has meticulously studied Stalin's Russia. Her book, *Gulag: A History*, narrates the history of the Soviet concentration camps system and describes his daily life in such camps. It makes extensive use of recently opened Russian archives, as well as various memoirs and interviews. *Gulag: A History* won the 2004 Pulitzer Prize for non-fiction, as well as Britain's Duff-Cooper Prize. The book was a finalist for the National Book Award, the National Book Critics Circle Award, the LA Times Book Award, and the Samuel Johnson Prize. It has appeared, or is due to appear, in more than two dozen translations, including all major East and West European languages. Speaking about the celebrated book at a lecture at the American Enterprise Institute on May 12, 2003, Applebaum said:

> Thanks to archives, we now know, for example that there were at least 476 camp systems, each one made up of hundreds, even thousands of individual camps or *lagpunkts,* sometimes spread out over thousands of square miles of otherwise empty tundra. We know that the vast majority of prisoners in them were peasants and workers, not the intellectuals who later wrote memoirs and books. We know that with a few exceptions, the camps were not constructed in order to kill people—Stalin preferred to use firing squads to conduct mass executions. Nevertheless they were, at times, very lethal: nearly one quarter of the Gulag's prisoners died during the war years. They were also very fluid: Prisoners left because they died, because they escaped, because they had short sentences, because they were being released into the Red Army or because they had been promoted, from prisoner

to guard. There were also frequent amnesties for the old, the ill, pregnant women, and anyone else no longer useful to the forced labor system. These releases were invariably followed by new waves of arrests.

As a result, between 1929, when they first became a mass phenomenon, and 1953, the year of Stalin's death, some 18 million passed through them. In addition, a further 6 or 7 million people were deported, not to camps but to exile villages. In total, that means the number of people with some experience of imprisonment, in Stalin's Soviet Union, could have run as high as 25 million, about 15 per cent of the population.

This was the reality of what Nehru called a "new civilization". Stalin had converted his entire country into a prison. As Applebaum said, "In the Soviet Union of the 1940s, the decade the camps reached their zenith, it would have been difficult, in many places, to go about your daily business and not run into prisoners."

In the Soviet Union, where Nehru thought "the future is full of hope", the bureaucrats and guards of concentration camps did not regard the inmates as fellow citizens, not even as human beings. According to Applebaum:

> In fact, this was an extremely powerful ideological combination—the disregarding of the humanity of prisoners, combined with the overwhelming need to fulfill the Plan. And nowhere is this clearer than in the camp inspection reports, submitted periodically by local prosecutors, and now kept neatly on file in the Moscow archives. When I first began to read them I was shocked, at first, both by their frankness and by the peculiar kind of outrage they express. Describing conditions in Volgolag, a railroad construction camp in Tatarstan in July 1942, one inspector complained, for example, that: "the whole population of the camp, including free workers, lives off flour. The only meal for prisoners is so-called 'bread' made from flour and water, without meats or fats." As a result, the inspector went on indignantly, there were high rates of illness, particularly scurvy—and, not surprisingly, the camp was failing to meet its production norms.

So much for the future that Nehru thought was "full of hope". It's not that communist barbarity was unknown to the outside world. As Applebaum said:

> In fact, in the 1920s, a great deal was known in the West about the bloodiness of Lenin's revolution. Western socialists, many of whose brethren had been jailed by the Bolsheviks, protested loudly and strongly against the crime of the Russian revolution. In the 1930s, however, as Americans became more interested in learning how socialism could be applied here, the tone changed. Writers and journalists went off to the USSR, trying to learn lessons they could use at home. The *New York Times* employed a correspondent, Walter Duranty, who lauded the five-year plan and argued, against all evidence, that it was a massive success—and won a Pulitzer Prize for doing so. Throughout the 1930s and 1940s, a part of the Western Left struggled to explain and sometimes to excuse the camps, and the terror, which created them, precisely because they wanted to try some aspects of the Soviet experiment at home. In 1936, after millions of Soviet peasants had died of famine, and millions more were in camps or in exile, the British socialists Sidney and Beatrice Webb published a vast survey of the Soviet Union, which explained, among other things, how the "downtrodden Russian peasant is gradually acquiring a sense of political freedom".

Jawaharlal Nehru was little different from the Webbs and other Leftists; he too chose to either ignore or deny the unpleasant aspects of socialism. Quite obviously, he must have dubbed—as communists did—such horror stories as "bourgeois propaganda".

Fortunately, unlike Stalin and Mao, Nehru was neither relentless nor bloodthirsty. Perhaps it was his association with Gandhi that ensured that he never used brute force to implement socialism. For instance, he did not collectivize agriculture as had been done in Bolshevik Russia and Red China. He did insist on "joint farming"; he preferred "relatively small co-operatives comprising one or two or three villages". His predilection for planning also led to the excessive controls in agriculture, as also in other sectors of the economy. But, as he wrote in an article in *National Herald*

(October 3, 1957), "I have no doubt that joint farming, wherever possible and agreed to, will be good, but it must be clearly understood that this can be no imposition and can only be brought in by the agreement of the parties."

The results of Nehruvian socialism were not barbarous or catastrophic, like in Russia and China. It did not end up in killing millions, but it surely arrested and subverted India's economic growth and led to a bleak economic future for at least two successive generations; even 58 years after Independence. This is reflected in India per capita income of $600, even 58 years after Independence, whereas small and less-endowed nations like South Korea and Taiwan boasted of per capita incomes in excess of $14,000. Socialism in India has created rot, chaos, and rampant cynicism. Worse, it has spawned an essentially parasitic intellectual class that thrives on this discredited ideology. This class infests academia, and much of the opinion-making apparatus. It has vitiated the education system and perverted public discourse. It is the biggest roadblock the nation is facing in the path to progress. Nowhere does this class make its obnoxious presence felt as vociferously as at state-coddled institutions such as the Delhi-based Jawaharlal Nehru University, inarguably the most Left-infested institution in the country.

The same intellectual class remains wedded to another leitmotif of Nehruvian ideology: anti-Americanism. Such is the hypocrisy and duplicity of intellectuals that while they secretly desire to go to America—for studying or teaching, as both activities increase their market value in India—they are also the loudest in their denunciation of the US for its real and imaginary sins. It would not be an exaggeration to say that Nehru himself was not as anti-American as are his ideological and political progeny. In fact, his anti-Americanism can also be seen as a consequence of his fascination for the Soviet Union. Not surprisingly, the Non-Aligned Movement, of which Nehru was one of the progenitors, always had a pro-Soviet and anti-US tilt. Under his successors, the tilt became more prominent. In short, we can say that Nehruvian socialism had strong links with non-alignment.

The period in which Nehru's postulates, thoughts, beliefs, and ideas were being formed—the early decades of the twentieth century—was the era in which socialism exerted a strong influence on the minds of many world leaders, especially leaders of newly independent countries. So, his fascination for socialism was not surprising. What is surprising is that Nehru so decisively turned his back on the English tradition.

For few contemporary Indians were as Anglicized as he was. He had lived in England, and had imbibed many of English values and ideals. Indeed, he has been called—by his admirers and detractors alike—the "last Englishman" to have ruled India. Yet, he gave up the most important concept of Anglican liberty and embraced the idea of French or Gallican liberty. The great twentieth century philosopher, Fredrich Hayek, made the contradistinction between the two concepts of liberty:

> . . . development of a theory of liberty took place mainly in the eighteenth century. It began in two countries, England and France. The first of these [Anglican] knew liberty; the second [Gallican] did not.
>
> As a result, we have had to the present day two different traditions in the theory of liberty: one empirical and unsystematic, the other speculative and rationalistic—the first based on an interpretation of traditions and institutions which had spontaneously grown up and were but imperfectly understood, the second aiming at the construction of a utopia, which has often been tried but never successfully. Nevertheless, it has been the rationalistic, plausible, and apparently logical argument of the French tradition, with its flattering assumptions about the unlimited powers of human reason, that has progressively gained influence, while the less articulate and less explicit tradition of English freedom has been on the decline.

Hayek is not very accurate when he talks about "the less articulate and less explicit tradition of English freedom". For the English tradition has been extremely articulate and explicit, as evident from the writings of major philosophers and writers. And it was in

the Anglo-Saxon tradition that the prerequisites of the modern world and its unprecedented prosperity were fashioned: individual liberty, limited government, and market economy. The marriage between liberty and order was made possible by the Anglo-Scottish enlightenment.

It is normally believed that Edmund Burke was the father of conservatism, and rightly so. However, it would be more appropriate to see him as somebody who articulated and defined Britishness, which epitomizes conservatism. Conservatism permeates British life, letters, philosophy, and attitude. It is present in empiricism as well as skepticism, the dominant streams of Anglo-Saxon philosophy. Locke is known as one of the founders of classical liberalism, but then it is little different from conservatism (It is only in the contemporary world that conservatives and liberals are in the opposing camps, with the latter leaning towards the Left).

The great skeptic, David Hume, adumbrated conservatism and specifically targeted Continental rationalism, especially that of Descartes. While Descartes generates his philosophy from an indubitable cogito or intellect, Hume was disdainful of intellect-oriented systems. In *An Enquiry Concerning Human Understanding*, Hume criticized Continental philosophers for considering "man in the light of a reasonable rather than an active being, and endeavor to form his understanding more than cultivate his manners. They regard human nature as a subject of speculation . . . They think it a reproach to all literature, that philosophy should not yet have fixed, beyond controversy, the foundation of morals, reasoning, and falsehood, vice and virtue, beauty and deformity, without being able to determine the source of these distinctions. While they attempt this arduous task, they are deterred by no difficulties; but proceeding from particular instances to general principles, they still push on their enquiries to principles more general, and rest not satisfied till they arrive at those original principles, by which in every science, human curiosity must be bounded . . . ."

The fact that Hume's enquiry was published in 1748, exactly a century before the "Communist Manifesto", underlines the pre-

science of this great skeptic. Hume's and other British authors' critiques of abstract ideologies immeasurably enriched the Anglo-Saxon tradition.

Unfortunately for India, Nehru deserted the Anglo-Saxon tradition and flirted with the ideas that conjured up a socialist utopia. In this, as noted earlier, he was not alone. In the twentieth century, almost every politician in India undermined this great tradition. We became the biggest importers of ideologies, especially the Left-leaning ones; there is no ideology—from emotive nationalism to communism to Fabian socialism—that has not reached the Indian shores. Besides, we had a good manufacturing base of our own—the pathologies of Gandhism, Sarvodaya, Swadeshi, Naxalism, etc. There is no other country in the world that can boast of so many ideologies. Worse, many of the ideologies have been implemented. Which makes India the most ideologically complicated country in the world.

Had Nehru not turned his back on the Anglo-Saxon tradition, had he tempered his enthusiasm for socialism with empiricism and skepticism—the two essentially distinctive features of the English tradition—he might have grown into a better scholar and a much greater leader, nation-builder, and statesman. Socialism corrupted him, as it corrupted myriad other fine men in the twentieth century. And this led to the squandering away of an unprecedented and unbroken political mandate the people of India so generously gave him during the formative decades of Independent India.

5 Khushwant Singh
A Liberal Fascist

Khushwant Singh is probably the most widely read author in India. A critically acclaimed litterateur, historian, and journalist, he has the rare quality of conveying his thoughts without taking recourse to jargon or holier-than-thou posturing. His two-volume *History of the Sikhs* is a critically acclaimed landmark work on the subject.

Unlike Arundhati Roy, Singh is erudite; so his writing is backed with some degree of authority. But when it comes to religion and, in particular, Islam, he trips; he starts pontificating; he gets lost in the crowd of clichés and shibboleths; worse, he simply echoes the falsehoods that reverberate in our climate of opinion. Let's begin with his views on religion.

He expounded his views on the subject in an essay, *Need for a New Religion in India.* As the name of the essay suggests, Singh makes little distinction between religion and everyday utilities; we *need* religion as much as, presumably, we *need* houses, clothes, cars, telephones, etc. He falls prey to what Friedrich A Hayek calls "constructivism"—that is, "the innocent sounding formula that, since man has himself created the institutions of society and civilization, he must also be able to alter them at will so as to satisfy his desires or wishes." Singh seems to derive his theory from the famous Marxian dictum that religion is the opium of the people; the natural corollary, according to Singh, is that if opium can be used

for evil purposes—and religion is mostly evil—it can also be used for good purposes. What is true for medical science should also be true for political science.

The essentials of the new faith he would like to set up are utilitarian. "My new religion for India would be primarily based on the work ethic. We have an apt motto which needs to be put into effect: *araam haraam hai* [a relaxed life is sinful]. It will provide leisure-time to recoup energy to resume work which yields material benefits." So far so good. But then Singh says, "Laws must be passed to limit the right to leave property to descendants and begging must be outlawed." A curious demand coming from a liberal (and one who has himself inherited a great deal of wealth).

For, in the first place, as far as inheritance is concerned, it is the right of the owner of property how he dispenses with it after his death, and *not* the right of the beneficiary. As American author Nathaniel Branden wrote, "In considering the issue of inherited wealth, one must begin by recognizing that the crucial right involved is not that of the heir but of the original *producer* of the wealth."

Second and more important, there is an invariable relationship between liberty and property in any society; one can't exist without the other. No less a thinker than John Locke, one of the pillars of liberal thought and a formulator of democratic processes, has written about the importance of the linkage between the two. In *An Essay Concerning the True Original, Extent and End of Civil Government*, he reaches the conclusion:

> But though men when they enter into society give up equality, liberty and executive power they had in the state of nature into the hands of the society, to be so far disposed of by the legislative as the good of the society shall require; yet it being only with an intention in everyone to *preserve* himself, his liberty and *property* (for no rational creature can be supposed to change his condition with an intention to be worse), the power of the society, or legislative constituted by them can never be supposed to extend farther than the common good, but is *obliged to secure everyone's property* by providing against those three defects

above-mentioned that made the state of nature so unsafe and uneasy . . . [emphasis added]

This is not merely political philosophy or abstract theory; India has learnt the truth of this lesson at its own expense. When the founding fathers of our republic authored the Constitution, they incorporated the right to property as a fundamental right. Within three decades of the Constitution, this right was downgraded; now, it is merely a legal right. It is pertinent to note here that the mutilation of the Constitution was primarily the work of the Leftists: politicians of socialist persuasion who took recourse to populist measures such as land reform through legislatures; their intellectual apologists who provided legitimacy to such measures; academics, press, all other means of influencing public opinion which were infiltrated with radicals. And while all this was happening, liberals like Khushwant Singh were either mute spectators to or willing accomplices in the creation of a climate of opinion against property. They never realized that true liberalism without the right to property is like an omelet without eggs.

It is not only on property that Singh is in agreement with the Left. Let's go back to his "new religion." Actually, this seems to be a quixotic exercise in social engineering—that bane of the twentieth century. Apparently, Singh wants, if it were possible, to legislate a new society.

To begin with, astrology should be "banned by legal enactment", otherwise it would continue to govern the lives of people to their detriment. Then, he would also ban "*shikar* [hunting] and the trapping of birds and animals". Further, "family planning must be made an integral part of our religion" (Reading this essay, one sometimes get confused whether Singh wrote about a new religion or a new constitution). Again, "the preservation of our environment must also become an essential part of our religion." Here he also suggests interference in religious affairs, something that has caused so much bloodshed and trouble in the past, the revolt of 1857 being a prime example. But then Singh does not seem to be aware of—at least, he does not subscribe to—the law of unintended consequences. Otherwise, he would not have suggested

another ban on the Hindu-Sikh custom of cremating the dead on funeral pyres. One wonders if Singh is a liberal or a fascist. Arguably, 'liberal fascist' is the right term.

In tune with fashionable environmentalism, he offers a green faith: "At every religious ceremony, be it the thread-ceremony, baptism, marriage or death, provision should be made for planting of forests."

Singh tries to customize and trivialize religion because he does not seem to know much about it, otherwise he would not have written in his essay on new religion: "Every religion has its own name and concept of God. He is Jehovah, Ishwar, Parmatma, Rabb, Khuda, Allah and Wahguru . . . . However, different the ways of conceiving Him, what all religions have in common are the powers they attribute to Him. He is the Creator, Preserver and Destroyer. He is Omniscient (all-knowing), Omnipotent (all-powerful) and Omnipresent; He is just, benign and merciful to the faithful and at the same time an angry God who metes out dire punishment to transgressors . . . ."

Singh has got it all wrong, for the way he has described God is not a universal way; this is the Judaic-Christian concept of God, as John Hick calls it in his authoritative *Philosophy of Religion*. Further, the concepts of Judaic-Christian God and, say, Ishwar are not identical or even similar. According to Hick, "God is conceived in the Judaic-Christian tradition as the infinite, self-existent Creator of everything else that exists. In this doctrine, creation means far more than fashioning new forms from an already given material (as a builder makes a house, or a sculptor at statue); it means creation out of nothing—*creatio ex nihilo*—the summoning of a universe into existence when otherwise there was only God." God says, "Let there be light," and there is light. As Hick puts it in technical terms, "God has absolute ontological independence." Needless to say, Hick's analysis of God and religion is correct.

In Hinduism, however, there is no unanimity of views on the forms—or even the existence—of Ishwhar. The Sankhya school of thought denies the existence of Ishwar, while the Vaisheshika school gives arguments for his existence. However, Ishwar does not enjoy absolute ontology; for Ishwar is said to be guided by the

Law of Karma. Besides, Ishwar does not create matter *ex nihilo*, as Judaic-Christian God does; Ishwar is co-eternal with matter.

It is amazing how a scholar of Khushwant Singh's stature fails to comprehend the nature and role of religion, finally agreeing with Leftists and other deracinated, secular intellectuals on the subject—that all religions are essentially the same. As Singh writes, "five items" are "generally regarded as the pillars of all religions: belief in God; reverence for the founders of religions; the status of scriptures; the sanctity accorded to places of worship and pilgrimage; and the use of prayer and ritual." He ignores that several schools of Buddhism and Jainism are atheistic; a more recent phenomenon is Marxism.

This is secular leveling of the phenomenon of religion; its myriad forms are made to look alike. Hick has most appropriately defined religion, by using Wittgenstein's concept of "language games", in terms of "family resemblances". According to Hick:

> In much religion there is the worship of a God or gods; but in Theravada Buddhism, for example, there is not. Again, religion often makes for social cohesion; yet in some strands it is aptly characterized as "what man does with his solitariness" (A. N. Whitehead). Again, religion often makes for the inner harmony of the individual; yet some of the greatest religious innovators seemed to their contemporaries to be unbalanced and even insane. The family resemblances model allows for such differences . . . .
>
> Within the ramifying set of family resemblances there is, however, one feature which is extremely widespread even though not universal. This is a concern with what is variously called salvation or liberation . . . . All the greatly developed world faiths . . . offer a transition from a radically unsatisfactory state to a limitlessly better one.

Interestingly, Khushwant Singh misses the essential feature of all religions, the concern called salvation. He fails to see that religion is the human response to the world—the world we live in, the world which is often beyond the ken of rational comprehension.

Religion gives meaning to the world, which otherwise seems so full of contradictions and unjustness; often, it gives a meaning to our lives. In the ultimate analysis, religion is rationalization *par excellence*. It explains the myriad injustices, contradictions, incongruities, paradoxes, and absurdities man faces on earth. Why are there wars, earthquakes, floods, famines, and other calamities, claiming so many innocent lives? Why are so many young lives cut short in accidents and crimes, whereas almost all politicians live long? Why do so many good people suffer? Why do scoundrels flourish? Why do so many people suffer from so many diseases? Why are some people born with congenital diseases? There are a large number of such questions which no philosopher or philosophy has been able to answer convincingly. Religion does offer answers; to some the answers may not be logically tenable or philosophically sound; but then ordinary people do not seek recondite syllogisms that impress logicians; people seek explanations that are simple as well as all-encompassing, taking care of all aspects of life. Religion mostly relies on—what logical positivist philosopher A.J. Ayer called—"unverifiable" principles and entities, the theory or karma and Christian God being two examples of unverifiable imperatives of religion. Intellectuals may not like it, but religion regulates our lives in more ways than it is recognized by them. Our festivals and carnivals, celebrations and mourning, customs and rituals—all spring from our religious beliefs, molding the *modus vivendi* into the grammar of faith.

Singh's book, *The End of India*, is the result of the secular leveling of all religious phenomena. Published in 2003, it was written, in his own words, "in anguish, anger, and bouts of depression"; for "we have lost in Gujarat". Needless to say, "we" stands for secular parties, forces, individuals, etc; needless to say again that Godhra—the place where three score Rambhaktas were incinerated by Muslim fanatics, and which triggered off the Gujarat riots—does not find a mention in Singh's account. No Godhra, only Gujarat—this has become the leitmotif of Indian liberals, in the same fashion as Vietnam was for the Left in a bygone era. You talk to any liberal about the political situation, and he would start

chanting the Gujarat mantra, accompanied with myriad falsehoods.

The second essay of Singh's book, "The Sangh And Its Demons," begins with a modern falsehood:

> All religions have and continue to have bigots who give founders of their religion and their teachings a bad name. Christians had the inquisitors who burnt innocent men and women at the stakes as heretics. Muslims have their Islamic fraternities whose leaders pronounce fatwas condemning people to death, ordering women to shroud themselves in veils and imposing draconian rules of behavior on the community. Sikhs had their Bhindranwale who forbade men to dye or roll up their beards, women to wear saris or jeans or put bindis on their foreheads, and who said nasty things about dhotian-topian waaley—the Hindus. Not to be outdone, Hindus produced their own fanatics who condemn Christianity and Islam as alien religions, and while mouthing platitudes about being the most tolerant religion on earth, hound Christian missionaries and target Muslim places of worship for destruction. In the name of Shri Rama, they demolished the Babri Masjid in Ayodhya, and Gujarat represented the worst face of religious extremism.

Notice the religious leveling—"all religions". The problem with the intellectuals like Singh—and, of course, with the Left—is that they draw unwarranted and generalized conclusions from well-recognized truths and beliefs. For instance, "all men are equal" means that any political system or social order should treat all men as equal; that is, nobody should be discriminated against by the state or by the society on account of their creed, color, caste, or community. However, the Leftists and liberals derive unjustifiable conclusions from this belief, making it appear that in their equality, all men are entitled to equal remuneration, wealth, etc. Such conclusions are untenable and illegitimate. In fact, great philosophers and statesmen never drew such conclusions. Abraham Lincoln, for instance, once said that the Negro was *not* equal

to the whites; but he emphasized on the Negro's right to equality in the sense that he should have the unfettered right to endeavor.

In these politically correct times, leveling has increased its own scope; now religion has been included in its ambit. So, according to liberals like Khushwant Singh, all religions are equal; which implies that all religious communities are also "equal"; and, since all religious communities are equal, it is possible to see a pattern in *all* communities: there are good people who follow the essence of their respective faiths; and there are "bigots who give founders of their religion and their teachings a bad name." All this seems logical to the liberal; conclusions are drawn from givens; corollaries are derived from proven theorems. With mathematical certainty.

The fact, however, is that the liberal mind is unable or unwilling to see the fallacies of such syllogism. For, all religions are *not* equal. As we saw earlier, even with "family resemblances" there are certain fundamental, ontological differences between different religions, one being between the concepts of God in the Semitic tradition and Ishwar in the Indian tradition. Even between Semitic religions, there are such differences; for instance, *Bible* is not the word of God, while *Koran* is. Further, according to Christians, Jesus is the Son of God, while Islam explicitly rules out any relation between Allah and man. Since there are fundamental differences between various religions, there are also fundamental differences between religious communities. Liberals like Khushwant Singh keep chanting the mantra that religion is, and should, be the private affair of a person. But it is not so; quite regularly and inevitably, it becomes a public affair. When the Kumbh fair is held, the entire local administration is geared up to supervise the arrangements; when Kanwarias carry the Ganga water to their homes, traffic is diverted by the authorities, and often the public at large is put to great inconvenience; the fortunes of markets are linked with festivals like Diwali, Holi, and Christmas, and these festivals are linked with religious faith; subsidy is given to Haj pilgrims, which obviously impacts the public exchequer. Further, observance of conventions, rituals, and customs affects a whole

range of activities. During Navaratras, for instance, a number of restaurants do not serve non-vegetarian food; in Muslim countries and Muslim localities, the entire mode of social existence undergoes a change during the month of Ramzan. In fact, one finds hundreds of examples all around to dispel the notion that religion is and should be the private affair of an individual.

This implies that the nature of every religion matters; it molds its followers according to its central beliefs and doctrines, theology and mythology, conventions and traditions, customs and rituals. Intellectuals like Khushwant Singh may have little to do with religion and its baggage, but most adherents are not like that; consequently, their lives are invariably intertwined with the tenets of their faith, by the myths that emanate from the belief system, by the rituals and customs they follow as believers.

Therefore, if a religion is inherently violent, its followers are more likely to take recourse to terrorism; if the precepts of a religion explicitly instruct that women are inferior human beings, they can never expect gender justice in such a society; if the Book of a religion exhorts the faithful to vanquish and eliminate the unbelievers, the followers of that religion would definitely show belligerence and bigotry; if a religion is decidedly closed and unambiguously prohibits scholarly pursuits, its adherents are likely to live in a benighted sphere. On the other hand, the believers of religions which preach harmony and fairness, which open up the vistas of mind and spirit, which whet the cerebral appetite—the believers of such religions are more likely to be peace-loving, tolerant, fair, and intellectually inclined.

In other words, all religions are no more "equal" than all men are equal. All efforts at leveling, of religions as well as of men, are the result of inadequate understanding of the subject and invariably result into disastrous consequences. Let's see some of the consequences. In another essay, "Communalism—An Old Problem", in the same book, Singh writes:

> By encouraging regressive mullahs and orthodox leaders and treating Indian Muslims as a homogeneous mass, the Congress consigned the whole community to an intellectual and social

ghetto. The Muslim closed his mind, he withdrew into himself as a tortoise withdraws into its shell. This helped the BJP demonize the community.

This is a typical liberal view on Muslims, obviously in line with the attitude that Muslims and Islam are never responsible for anything; it is always imperialism, neo-imperialism, Orientalism, Hindu nationalism, or media bias that are the culprits. In this case, the culprit is the Grand Old Party, all this despite the fact that the Congress has always been accused of appeasing the Muslims— and rightly so, because whether it was under Mahatma Gandhi or Jawaharlal Nehru in the first half of the twentieth century, or under Rajiv Gandhi in the second half, the Congress always tried to woo Muslim political support. But in Khushwant Singh's scheme of things, the party becomes the main accused. And the accomplices? Well, the usual suspects, "regressive mullahs and orthodox leaders," as if they are parasitic entities on the body-politic of Islam, inconsistent with and hostile to its essential teachings. Khushwant Singh and other liberals seem incapable of understanding that the so-called "regressive mullahs and orthodox leaders" are the real representatives of Islam (as discussed in a separate chapter); and this is the reason that their hold over the community has survived the threats of Arabism (in the form of Baathism in the Arab world), secularism, and socialism.

Singh persists in the blame-somebody-else policy:

The Muslim attitude is not a political but a national problem. We did not do enough after 1947 to rehabilitate them in the national mainstream.

This is not correct. The Indian Constitution does not discriminate against anybody on the basis of caste community, creed, or ethnicity (though the Pakistan Constitution is explicitly discriminates against the minorities). There is nothing in any of India's laws and statutes that discriminates against Muslims. In fact, the Muslims, along with other religious minorities, are especially protected by institutions such as the Minorities Commission and the

National Human Rights Commission (NHRC). Singh may say that though there is nothing *on paper* that shows discrimination against the Muslims, the discrimination is in attitude and in practice; it pervades the climate of opinion; it subtly infects the polity, the culture, academics, and the media.

Let's begin with politics. Every political party is in the business of wooing Muslims, often at the expense of Hindus, a tendency that the BJP once denounced as minorityism. Later, the BJP also did the same thing—organizing Iftar get-togethers, placating Pakistan and Bangladesh, turning a Nelson's eye to the atrocities on Hindus in these countries. All major political parties champion the cause of Muslims, in Parliament and outside it. Three Muslims have been Presidents of the nation; one was Union home minister; many others have held important offices. Surely, in the political domain, there has been little discrimination.

In art and culture, a large number of Muslims have earned big money and won awards, often from the state. Cinema, painting, literature—Muslims are everywhere. Mohammad Rafi, Dilip Kumar, Meena Kumari, Aamir Khan, Shahrukh Khan, Javed Akhtar, M. F. Hussain—all of them are household names.

As far as academics and the media are concerned, we have seen in this chapter and others how our great intellectuals twist facts, distort truths, and peddle lies to misguide the people about the real nature of Islam. So, what else does Khushwant Singh wants us to do to "rehabilitate" the Muslims in the national mainstream? He talks as if the Muslims were the victims of Partition, whereas the fact is that they were responsible for it.

Again, he says:

> The non-Muslim has always had it deeply embedded in his mind that Muslims are bigots, fanatics and treacherous. We were brought up on tales of heroism of Prithviraj Chauhan, Maharana Pratap, Guru Gobind Singh and Chhatrapati Shivaji. All our heroes were non-Muslims who had fought Muslims. No one in our pantheon was Muslim. Akbar was just a token figure. We were exposed to evidence of what Muslim conquerors had done: dese-

crated our temples, massacred our citizenry and imposed humiliating taxes on them.

Singh is right: all Muslims are not bigots, fanatics, and treacherous. Further, our history has been distorted, by the Left as well as the Right. Yet, certain facts cannot be denied. Muslims did desecrate temples, massacre Hindu citizenry, and impose the jaziya. There is a mountain of evidence to confirm all this, dug out and presented by historian Sita Ram Goel (about whose work we shall discuss later). I would like to add that these facts should not be used to settle scores with Muslims in today's world. As for the heroism of Prithviraj Chauhan, Maharana Pratap, Chhatrapati Shivaji, and Guru Gobind Singh, the people of India appreciate them because they had the courage to take on the might of Muslims in the medieval period.

Fortunately, the people are much more sensible than intellectuals such as Khushwant Singh. People are accused of being prejudiced, but their prejudices are based on solid empirical evidence, for they believe in the sovereignty of sense perception—quite unlike the Indian liberals who blindly borrow from the Left. So, Singh jettisons empirical evidence, common sense, and reason to blindly follow Leftist theory. This is evident from the observations he makes—or, to be precise, the Leftist untruths he parrots—in the apocalyptically named, *The End of India*:

> If the Muslims killed and destroyed, the non-Muslims (the Rajputs, Jats, Marathas and Sikhs) did no less.
>
> When Brahminical Hinduism gained favor again [that is, when Buddhism ceased to be "on the ascendant in India"] with ruling dynasties, especially in the ninth and tenth centuries, Buddhists were persecuted and their places of worship demolished. Later, in the reign of many Muslim rulers, Hindus were discriminated against and their temples destroyed.
>
> The instigation [for communal riots] comes from the educated middle class of tradesmen (incidentally, the constituency of the BJP) and politicians (except perhaps the communists).

> If they [Muslims] are foreigners, we all are. The only people who are indigenous are the adviasis, whom we have all but made extinct.
>
> I attribute much of the blame for the resurgence of Hindu fundamentalism to serials on the *Ramayana* and the *Mahabharata*.

Khushwant Singh goes on and on, echoing the weird theories, fantasies, and myths spread by the Left, further muddying the already perverted public discourse. He reminds one of *Euthyphro*, one of the famous dialogues of Plato. In this dialogue, Socrates chides Euthyphro for his cocksureness: "You are languid through your affluence in wisdom."

Thanks to his languor, Singh is unwilling to see through the subterfuge of the Left. For instance, how it creates confusion in scales. The depredations of Muslims, and the scale of such depredations, are too well-known to be repeated; yet, the Left mixes them with stray and sporadic violence perpetrated by non-Muslims against Muslims; and Singh languidly accepts the lie, saying non-Muslims "did no less."

Despite all his scholarship, experience, age, and exposure, Khushwant Singh repeatedly falls prey to the liberals vice: And he unquestioningly follows the Left.

6 Kuldip Nayar
Banality *par excellence*

There are some people in India who go lyrical when discussing Hindu-Muslim relations and India-Pakistan ties. They start waxing eloquent about the magnificent diversity of India, the Bhakti poets and Sufi saints, and the syncretic traditions. They start quoting the Buddha and Guru Nanak, Gandhi and Nehru. And in this syrupy and sloppy extravaganza, they lose contact with reality. Kuldip Nayar is among such sentimentalists whose flights of fancy keep them in the rarefied realms of multiculturalism and liberal claptrap—at a safe distance from the actual world.

And, like many other liberals, Nayar does not want to face the real world; it appears dreadful and incomprehensible. Instead, he seeks refuge in apocalyptic banality, as in an article, "For Tomorrow, Remain Together: The Spectre of Division Chases Us into the New Year," in *The Indian Express* (December 31, 2002):

> Gujarat shook us to the roots. First, Godhra happened. Then the bloodshed at Godhra was shamelessly used to unify the Hindu majority as if they were under threat from Muslim extremists and Pakistan. We are being dragged once again into the fires of the Hindu-Muslim divide.
>
> Communal polarization is too horrible a prospect to compre-

> hend in a country that is already divided on the basis of caste, language, region and standard of living. Anti-minority forces are not new. They were there even before Independence. You have only to think of the Kolkata and Bihar riots in the late forties. Mahatma Gandhi and Jawaharlal Nehru fought them effectively. Their discourse was different. They were clear in their mind that one nationality and one religion were not synonymous. Gandhi said: "The Hindus, the Mohammedans, the Parsis and the Christians who have made this their country are fellow countrymen and they will have to live in unity if only in their own interest."

This passage exposes Nayar as a person who has little understanding of the condition of India, and yet he is hard-bent on sermonizing. He can't see the Gujarat riots in their proper perspective; the riots took place because people at large had lost faith in the State machinery; the Hindu community donned the mantle of the State to punish the guilty; but, since a community or society does not enjoy the paraphernalia, mechanism, or expertise of the State, the result in such situations is always indiscriminate violence and widespread chaos. The Modi government failed primarily in preventing the society from assuming the role of the State; for, the assumption of such a role by any society is the first step towards barbarianism. Civilization is, after all, all about keeping mass passions and mob depredations in check. Nayar and other intellectuals allege that the Modi government organized "pogrom" against Muslims. According to *Merriam-Webster's Dictionary*, a "pogrom" is "an organized massacre of helpless people: specifically, such a massacre of Jews." There were no pogroms, though violence against the Muslims did take place, and such violence was the result of widespread anti-Muslim feeling. There may or may not have been involvement of some elements of the State machinery, but there were no pogroms.

Liberals like Nayar are loath to look into the reasons why such violent emotions are aroused against Muslims. Why is it that in today's world, it is mostly the Muslims who have major problems everywhere? They have problems with Jews; their undying hatred

for Israel is indicative of that. They have problems with Christianity; Muslim leaders accuse them of launching crusades against Islam. And in India, of course, there are the odious Hindu communalists. The Muslims are against America; September 11 was a reminder of the fact. They are against Europe, which is accused of not respecting Islamic traditions; the scarf issue in France is a recent example. They are also against China, as Beijing is discovering in its eastern province of Sinkiang. They attack Moscow.

But why do only Muslims have problems? There are Hindus, Buddhists, Christians, Sikhs, Parsis, and Jews all over the world, but why is it only the Muslims who indulge in violence? Nayar, like other liberals, would not like to answer any of these questions; instead, he takes recourse to clichéd lamentation:

> We find that there are people who even abuse Gandhi and all that he stood for. The future looks gloomy because not many dare to challenge those in power. To see the communalists prospering deepens our disgust. The Dalits have never been given their due. But we were beginning to believe that the various laws and affirmative action through reservations had made a dent in the thick wall of discrimination, though they couldn't pull it down altogether. But the Haryana killings, with the connivance of the authorities [there were reported atrocities in Haryana], have punctured our confidence. Dalits are still humiliated, beaten or killed at will by the upper castes. One may not like Mayawati's government in Uttar Pradesh in many ways but hers is the only state where Dalits have the confidence that the wrong done to them will not go unpunished.
>
> Never before had one heard about corruption in the judiciary so persistently as in this year. Two successive chief justices of India have admitted this.

What's wrong in questioning Gandhi's wisdom (or, for that matter, in questioning anybody's wisdom)? Such questioning does not make him small. It would do injustice to Gandhi himself if we blindly accepted whatever "he stood for". For instance, Gandhi once called Parliament a "prostitute". He was against most mate-

rial progress and economic development all of us work for; he was against science and technology; such Gandhian legacy is still a bane of the economy. There is nothing wrong in critiquing Gandhi, or any other national icon.

Nayar has accepted Leftist theory, according to which Hindu society is the most rigid, iniquitous, and barbarous in the world, offering no succor or scope to the Dalits; despite all policies and programs, they "are still humiliated, beaten or killed at will by the upper castes". In this rambling discourse, the judiciary becomes the next target. This is followed by self-mortification:

> After 55 years we should have developed some ethics of governance if not of our behavior as communities. Tyrants have sprouted at all levels. Their swagger is based on their proximity to the seat of power. They increasingly flaunt, not only their contacts, but also their bigotry.
>
> At the end of the year one finds that the desire for self-preservation has become the sole motivation for actions and behavior. The only anxiety is to survive at any cost. In a situation like this, it is not surprising if values begin to count for less and less.
>
> The most dangerous thing about this situation is that we are on the brink of losing our pluralistic image and values. Many people have now been brainwashed into thinking that "Hindutva" will do everything for us. It won't. The design for living is not the raised, but the outstretched, hand. Love, not hate. Friendship, not enmity.
>
> India is home to so many kinds of people. The country has all religions and cultures. People here have to live together in friendship and harmony. There is no other way. As the Israeli poet, Yehuda Amichai, says in one of his poems, "If we don't remain together, we won't remain at all."

It goes without saying that for Kuldip Nayar the "tyrants"—who are sprouting at all levels and who flaunt their "contacts" and "bigotry"—include only the likes of Narendra Modi and Uma Bharti; such harsh descriptions escape, say, Mayawati who has

given the Dalits "the confidence that the wrong done to them will not go unpunished." This about a politician who respects neither the law of the land nor the restraints of decency and convention, whose corruption is matched only by her brazenness, who added the dimension of vituperation to the political discourse.

In a way, this is a typical instance of liberal intellectual duplicity: blast the Right, go soft on the Left-tilting politicians. It is an easy option: a liberal knows that he can safely lambaste Narendra Modi, L.K. Advani, or Praveen Togadia; but if he chooses to criticize the Laloo Prasad Yadavs or the Mayawatis with equal vehemence, he is likely to attract considerable criticism, not only from the targeted politicians or his cronies, but also from Leftwing sages. And the intellectuals, like the sheep in Orwell's *Animal Farm*, will provide the chorus. In fact, the worst possible calamity can strike you: you may be called a communal person, a fascist, a closet knickerwallah—the ultimate insult.

Nayar, obviously, does not want to earn the ire of secular politicians and eminent intellectuals. He wants to please them, and he does so by peddling half-truths and untruths. This he did in an article, "In Dhaka, Delhi on the Mind: It Is Time We Stopped Treating Bangladesh As a Poor Relation," in *The Indian Express* (January 8, 2003):

> At Dhaka no one takes Deputy Prime Minister L. K. Advani's assertion that there are 20 million Bangladeshis in India seriously. It is considered part of the BJP's political propaganda to heighten Hindu suspicions against the Indian Muslim in order to garner votes. There is, however, a feeling that secularism in India has eroded over the last few years. More disconcerting is the growing conviction that the doings of the ruling BJP are justifying Mohammad Ali Jinnah's two-nation theory.

Nayar reports the *views* of the Dhaka elite as if they were well-known *facts* and as if Advani's assertion were part of the BJP's diabolical "political propaganda to heighten Hindu suspicions against the Indian Muslim." The great journalist has little to say about the collusion of the Dhaka elite in the perpetration of atroci-

ties on Hindus. He has even less to say about illegal Bangladeshi migrants; presumably, he blindly accepts the Khaleda Zia regime's lie that there are no illegal Bangladeshi migrants in India. And he ignores the simple fact: more than 20 million illegal Bangladeshis are in India, millions of them are residing in Delhi itself, the city Nayar lives in. Millions of illegal Bangladeshis live in the localities of trans-Yamuna Delhi as also on the bank of the Yamuna. But Nayar is too good a liberal to rely on empirical evidence; he would listen to the command of Leftist Theory rather than submit to the sovereignty of sense perception.

It is pertinent to notice here that even as intellectuals and Left-wing theoreticians downplay or debunk the threat of Bangladeshi infiltration, communists in power in West Bengal regard demographic aggression by the eastern neighbor as a great threat. At the state chief ministers' conference in Delhi in early February in 2003, the two CPI(M) chief ministers from West Bengal and Tripura—Buddhadev Bhattacharya and Manik Sarkar—echoed the views of the hated Sangh Parivar. Bhattacharjee said: " . . . on the question of dealing with illegal infiltrators from Bangladesh, our state government is in agreement with the government of India that whenever such infiltration is detected, the foreign nationals should be pushed back forthwith." Sarkar also expressed similar views, suggesting that every Bangladeshi was an ISI agent. He asserted that the ISI, and "possibly Al Qaeda", were operating from Bangladesh.

Nayar, however, has nothing to do with such facts. He blindly accepts the Bangladesh government's viewpoint. And the "feeling" in Dhaka is that "secularism in India has eroded over the last few years". Nayar feels the same way. He does not have a word of criticism for the Dhaka elite, which has been a mute spectator to, if not an active colluder in, the myriad carnages against Hindus in Bangladesh. But when it comes to the Gujarat carnage, he loses all sense of proportion:

> Since the Gujarat carnage, the belief in Bangladesh is that it is only a question of time before India became a Hindu state for all practical purposes. The Hindu population in Bangladesh, which

> constitutes roughly 12 per cent of some 150 million people, feels tense and blames the rulers at New Delhi (the erstwhile NDA government) for spoiling the communal harmony, which was limping back to near normalcy after the demolition of the Babri masjid. Still there is no doubting the fear of Muslim fanatics, who have the support of the Jamaat-e-Islami, a partner in the Khaleda Zia government.

Notice how cleverly Nayar shifts all blame of anti-Hindu activities in Bangladesh to "the rulers in New Delhi". So, it is the murderous BJP functionaries in India who are responsible for "spoiling the communal harmony, which was limping back to near normalcy after the demolition of the Babri masjid". In other words, it is the bigoted Hindus and their more bigoted leaders who are responsible for every anti-Hindu atrocity in Bangladesh; they demolish Babri Masjid at Ayodhya, leading to killings in Bangladesh; they kill Muslims in Gujarat, and, therefore, Hindus are justifiably butchered in Bangladesh: it is always the Hindus who pull the trigger.

Nayar is trying to pass off a white lie as an acceptable truth: that Hindus are at the root cause of every Hindu-Muslim dispute. It is a lie because facts show that the nature of Islam is responsible for all disputes between Muslims and non-Muslims (as demonstrated in the chapter on Islam).

Nayar himself says that there are 12 per cent Hindus in Bangladesh. At the time of Partition, there were about 30 per cent Hindus. So, by his own admission, millions of Hindus have been either massacred or forced to convert to Islam or flee to India. Most of these atrocities clearly happened before December 6, 1992, the day when Babri Masjid was demolished. How do you explain that, Mr. Nayar? The history of Bangladesh, which was earlier East Pakistan, is the history of discrimination against and slaughter of Hindus; can everything be blamed on "the rulers in New Delhi"?

In Nayar's scheme of things, New Delhi is responsible for every possible evil in Bangladesh:

> [Some economists] believe that it is in India's own interest to ensure that Bangladesh got business openings. What they meant was that if New Delhi had encouraged Indian investments in Bangladesh, as it had promised soon after the country's freedom in 1971—some joint plans were also formulated by the two nations—it would have developed the country economically to the extent that people would have found enough opportunities to keep them rooted in their own country.

Thus, according to Nayar, India is to be blamed even for the Bangladesh's economic backwardness! The article ends on an outrageous note:

> Foreign Minister Morshed Khan denies that Bangladesh has any training camps for insurgents. He also says that the presence of ISI is a figment of the imagination. He is ready to allow Indian inspection without notice. But a former minister in the Sheikh Hasina government disagrees. The ISI has always operated from Bangladesh, he says. Now more than ever before.

This is typical liberal even-handedness: juxtapose two opposing statements, without giving your own view. Nayar does not offer any opinion on the matter, but the tone and tenor of his article is clear: India in general and the Hindus in particular are responsible for all that is wrong in Bangladesh.

Since his understanding of the situation is essentially flawed, its little surprise that the solutions he suggests are silly. What he recommends is total capitulation by India, the biggest country in south Asia:

> And, at one time, it looked as if New Delhi had found a formula, the Gujral Doctrine—going more than halfway to accommodate neighbors in order to remove their mistrust. But the BJP-led government has destroyed most of the formula. Electoral politics has had the better of the government. An anti-Muslim stance to garner the vote of Hindus seems to be at the back of its tough stand

towards Islamabad and Dhaka. This has only deepened the mistrust of the neighbors.

The "one time" Nayar remembers so nostalgically was when I.K. Gujral was India's prime minister (It may also be remembered that Gujral had made Nayar India's high commissioner in London). Gujral, a Left-liberal of Nehruvian vintage, formulated a policy for south Asia the essential feature of which was limitless appeasement of neighboring nations—as Nayar says, "going more than halfway to accommodate neighbors in order to remove their mistrust." The policy was so imprudent and foolish that even many liberal experts found it worth discarding; but Nayar links up the abandoning of a thoughtless policy to the "anti-Hindu stance" of the BJP. However, the fact is that though the Vajpayee government technically dumped the Gujral Doctrine, it did not adopt an Indian version of the Monroe Doctrine; nor did the Vajpayee government give up appeasement, as evident from its pusillanimous reaction to the killing of about 15 men of India's Border Security Force (BSF) in Bangladesh in the middle of 2001. The unfortunate men had inadvertently entered the Bangladesh territory; they were tortured and then murdered in cold blood by the men of Bangladesh Rifles. All newspapers carried the picture of a BSF soldier's body tied to a rod, which was being carried by two Bangladeshis—the way people carry hunted beasts. The entire nation was incensed, but not the Vajpayee regime, which routinely "condemned" the outrage as if it had happened to Colombian cops rather than to Indian soldiers!

In other words, appeasement continues unabated and undiminished, but Nayar is not satisfied: nothing less than total capitulation by India to its neighbors would please him. All this is in tune with Leftist thinking. Not surprisingly, he wrote:

> The Iraq war should have been a wake-up call for India—to shake off its lethargy which has made our foreign policy moribund. After having failed to raise the issue of morality during the Iraq war, New Delhi should have taken the initiative after the hostilities to make the countries of the region—from Afghanistan

to Myanmar—realize the necessity of acting in concert to uphold their regional identity and independence . . .

The purpose should be how to resist the pressure of the Anglo-American axis which may want the region to conform to certain pet ideas it has nourished. Now we either hang together or be hanged separately.

Needless to say, in his scheme of things "morality" means complete ignorance of national security. What is this "Anglo-American axis"? And what are its "pet ideas"? Clearly, there is no such formal arrangement that can be called an Anglo-American axis; the arrangement is in the conspiracies that the Left sees all around. And the so-called pet ideas are the ideas of capitalism and democracy that the entire West, and not just the US and the UK, favors in all over the world. In fact, gradually the entire world is moving towards capitalism and democracy; the history of the world since the collapse of the Soviet Union can be seen as the march from socialism to capitalism and dictatorship to democracy. The march goes on, much to the chagrin of the Left—and to the consternation of the Kuldip Nayars, who borrow from the Left. The Left wants the entire world to unite against the "imperialist" Anglo-American axis; Nayar also wants that:

Regional cooperation [in south Asia] does not come about by mere wishful thinking. It must be a matter of give and take. India will need to go far to accommodate suspicious of recalcitrant neighbors. New Delhi can demand that Islamabad must stop cross-border terrorism. But it cannot slam the door on the nationals of the neighboring countries or cut off all modes of communication. The Bangladeshis, too, feel that they are suspect in the eyes of Indians. No regional co-operation, much less an organization, can be built on the feeling that we Indians are always right.

Nayar's concept of "give and take" is easy to sum up: India should give and its neighbors should take. According to him, New Delhi can keep on asking Islamabad to stop cross-border terrorism—and do little else—but it should not "slam the door on the

nationals of neighboring countries". Pakistan trains, arms, aids, and abets terrorists against India; the terrorists massacre our citizens, bomb our cities, and attack our Parliament, but we should think only of "regional cooperation"!

Bangladesh lets loose an ethnic cleansing within it and a demographic aggression against India, lets the vicious ISI operate from its soil, and organizes pogroms against Hindus, but again we should be worried about regional cooperation! We should also ensure that there are "enough opportunities" in Bangladesh so that it does not indulge in demographic aggression!

But then this is the line of the Leftist intellectual: he screams every time—and such occasions are rare—when the Indian government shows slightest self-respect or self-interest. That Nayar blindly follows the Leftist line also becomes evident from another article:

> It is wrong to assume that the attack by terrorists in New York and Washington in September 2001 hardened America's tone and tenor. It was already acting as a tough and self-righteous country. The attack gave it a justification to suppress dissent, opposition or what it did not like in any part of the world. Increasingly, the US was seen trying to cure the symptom—terrorism—and not the disease—the grievance. Through economic, political and social ties it could have made nations more independent and more viable. But it was no do-gooder. It wanted the different countries to realize that America—and America alone—counted in the world.

How is America "a tough and self-righteous country"? How and when did it "suppress dissent, opposition or what it did not like"? Nayar doesn't explain all this; like Leftists, he only makes allegations, offering little evidence to support them. Again, like Leftists, he repeats the cliché that terrorism is merely the "symptom", while the disease is "grievance". What grievances? No answers. Whose grievances? No answers. What was the grievance of Mohammad Atta and his fellow terrorists responsible for September 11?

Liberals like Nayar fail to realize that by projecting terrorism as a symptom or outcome of something more hideous—be it grievance or poverty—they are merely projecting the terrorists as victims, if not martyrs. And the victims seem like villains—America in the case of September 11, for instance.

It is not just Leftist politics that Nayar accepts unquestioningly but also its economics. In an article, "Enrons of the Rich World" (rediff.com, April 9, 2001), he wrote:

> True, the multinationals can fill some gaps which India may not be able to do on its own in the near future. It is only a question of time. India has the potential—and manpower—to convert the country into an economic giant. But to barter independence for a pot of money has never been the nation's ethos. Its long struggle for freedom confirms that. In any case, some day some government will husband the resources to pull the country out of the mire of underdevelopment and set it on the road to progress.

This would seem straight from JNU. Notice the command economy principles: "some day some government . . . road to progress." It is only that government that can "set" the country on the road to progress—not the people, not the individual, not individual enterprise and endeavor, only "some government". Nayar borrows lock, stock, and barrel:

> Are the multinationals interested in making a quick buck or making the buyer feel he has not been exploited? Exploitation reminds us of the days of imperialism. It cannot be duplicated in the 21st century when countries have cast off slavery.
>
> This is the crux of problems facing developing countries. The G-8 nations, the rich nations, fail to appreciate this. They are going ahead with their old policy. They call it globalization, but it is an instrument to capture markets in the underdeveloped or developing countries for the goods which the West cannot sell in its developed world. Protests outside the venue of earlier G-8 meetings should have made them wiser. But they did not. Consequently, thousands of protesters marched in the streets of Genoa,

Italy, where the G-8 nations recently met, to express their resentment against global development strategy.

What happened at Genoa? It looked like urban war zones after the initially peaceful protests broke down into riotous confrontations. Small groups clad in black, torched cars and smashed shops as larger columns of organized protestors marched on the barricades protecting the port area where leaders of the group of eight industrialized nations opened a three-day summit. The conflict crossed an ominous threshold with the death of one demonstrator—the first casualty in the wave of protests challenging the morality and standards of globalization that was launched at the December 1999 WTO summit in Seattle.

President Bush and his counterparts—the leaders of Britain, Canada, France, Germany, Italy, Japan and Russia—never saw the point of protests. The issue that moved people from across three continents to travel to Genoa was not whether to globalize, but how to do it in ways that would not leave the majority of people behind. The protests were demanding global justice on a wide range of issues, from debt relief for developing countries to lower barriers against immigration from poorer to richer countries. Will the G-8 do it or will they go on like Enron, from one project to another, bamboozling people and giving the impression that what was being done was in their interest? The answer to this question will give a peep into the strategy of the Enrons of the rich nations.

Reading such passages in articles by Kuldip Nayar, I feel that at least he could have rehashed the articles and changed the language. The same old Leftist bogeys of "imperialism" and "exploitation", the familiar shibboleths of rich nations capturing markets of poor nations, the usual lionization of "protestors" who are normally the professional mourners. Unsurprisingly, the rambling rhetoric comes up with the familiar denunciation of multinational corporations—"the Enrons of the world."

Kuldip Nayar's flight from reality continues unabated. Witness the complete disconnect between his notions and the Bangladesh situation. Even the Left Front government of West Bengal would not be willing to accept his arguments and assertions.

7 Secularism
The Great Indian Fetish

Secularism is the most crucial subject in Indian politics: it is the ultimate frame of reference to commend or condemn parties and leaders; it is the subject most commented upon in the country. Yet, few in India know or understand what secularism *really* is.

As a consequence, the meaning of "secularism" has been debauched; it is perceived as synonymous with anything that is good, noble, or exalted. Concomitantly, "communalism" is taken as the antonym of secularism. If there is anything that excites India's liberal intellectuals, it is a debate on secularism. They are not only wrong in most of their assertions about secularism but actually widely of the mark. They begin with the abuse of language and end up subverting the grammar of public discourse. And that suits the Leftist intellectual just fine.

Philosophical problems, wrote Wittgenstein, arise when language goes on holiday. The same can be said about most political problems. So, let's see what do the words, secularism and communalism, *actually* mean. According to *Merriam-Webster's Dictionary*, the word "secular" means "of or relating to the worldly or temporal (~concerns)", "not overtly or specifically religious (~music)", "not ecclesiastical or clerical (~courts)", "not bound by monastic vows or rules; specifically, of, relating to, or forming clergy not belonging to a religious order or congregation." *The*

Compact Oxford Reference Dictionary defines "secular" as "not religious or spiritual" and "(of clergy) not subject to or bouned by religious rule". On the other hand, "communalism" means, according to www.wordreference.com, "loyalty and commitment to the interests of your own minority or ethnic group rather than to society as a whole" and "the practice of communal living and communal ownership". Therefore, in no way are the two words, "secularism" and "communalism", related, notwithstanding Indianism. And, again, in no way can the former be considered as synonymous with good, noble, or virtuous.

This is not a futile semantic exercise. It is well known that Stalin was responsible for the death of 40 million people; yet, he was secular. In fact, his secularism, a by-product of the Marxian dogma, was so aggressive that the erstwhile Soviet Union set up a museum of atheism. Nor does his secularism make Stalin a champion of religious harmony; his hatred for Jews is not the creation of any "bourgeois propaganda".

Mao was another great secularist, and another great butcher of the twentieth century. According to *Mao: The Unknown Story*, a recent book by Jung Chang and Jon Halliday, the Great Helmsman killed 70 million people. Ditto with Pol Pot of Cambodia. Pol Pot was also a secularist, who wanted to create a new society but ended up murdering every seventh citizen of his small south-east Asian country.

Among non-communist mass murderers, Hitler was the greatest. He killed six million Jews, but this was not because they were non-Christians; he got them eliminated because they belonged to what he thought was an "inferior race". But he also established his "secular credentials" by killing millions of Christians—Poles, Czechs, Russians, and members of other "inferior races"!

This is not to say that all secularists are violent people; what we assert is that being secular does not necessarily transform a man into an angel. Empirical evidence in India, too, bears out our contention that secularism has nothing to do with goodness or virtue. In Indian politics, we have scamsters and crooks on both sides of the so-called secular-communal divide.

Indian intellectuals believe that a number of our political and other problems are because of the weakening of secularism over the years. According to them, equal respect for and harmony between all religious groups depends on the success of secularism. They are wrong. What is really needed for peaceful coexistence between all religious groups—and for all other fruits of civilization—is *the rule of law*. It may be recalled that in the wake of September 11 attacks in the US and the July 7 bombings in London, there were no violent reprisals against Muslims, though both nations hardly qualify to be called secular. Great Britain is technically not secular, the monarch being the defender of the Anglican faith. The US President routinely invokes God in his speeches, and the god he invokes is the Christian God. Every currency note the US prints has "In God, we trust" inscribed on it.

India, on the other hand, is vociferously secular; all political parties, including the Bharatiya Janata Party (BJP), vie with each other to show themselves as secular. Political formations are made on the basis of secularism. Yet, there was a bloody outburst of public fury in the wake of Godhra incident in 2002, resulting in the death of hundreds of Muslims.

Further, there is no secular state in the Arabian peninsula; in Saudi Arabia, for instance, non-Muslims are not even allowed to practice their religions. Yet, no anti-Hindu reprisals were reported in the aftermath the demolition of Babri Masjid on December 6, 1992, or after the killing of Muslims in the Gujarat riots in 2002. Therefore, we can cogently assert that the necessary condition for religious harmony is the rule of law and not secularism.

It is quite evident that in India the rule of law has been considerably weakened, if not broken down altogether. One need not read Arun Shourie's book *Governance and the Sclerosis That Has Set In* to know that government is the biggest problem the country is facing today. Whether it is at the federal or the local level, the rot in governance is obvious. The terms we commonly use when describing government functioning are corruption, venality, incompetence, inefficiency, unimaginativeness, rigidity, red tape, callousness, apathy, etc.

The legislative branch of our democratic system is no better than the executive. It is rarely that meaningful debate takes place in Parliament or state assemblies. One would have expected eloquence of oration and cogency of arguments in Parliament of the world's largest democracy. What one comes across, however, is pandemonium, sloganeering, screaming, bad behavior, rambling speeches, and gross indiscipline. It is seldom that the nation's highest forum is used to enrich the public discourse. In recent years, the Opposition—whether it is the BJP or the Congress—has made a mockery of parliamentary democracy by routinely boycotting it. Parliamentary committees, purported to be a check on the executive, are rarely taken seriously by the honorable members of Parliament.

The third organ of the system, the judiciary, is also hardly a picture of efficiency and probity. A few years ago, an incumbent chief justice of the country observed that one-fifth of the lower judiciary was corrupt; needless to say, this is considered a conservative estimate. A visit to any district court is enough to shock anybody. There are millions of cases pending in our courts; it takes years to dispose of even the simplest of matters. Criminals walk free; the innocent poor defendants often face enormous harassment.

There are abundant signs of the weakening, if not complete breakdown, of the rule of law. However, our intellectuals are obsessed with secularism; it has blinded them to such an extent that they cannot even recognize the nature of problems India is facing, let alone help solve them; they confuse the rule of law with the existence of secularism.

Intellectuals are actually a deracinated lot; secularism is their magnificent castle in the air whose arches and domes they have fallen in love with; they abhor the idea of any connection with the ground realities, the realities of faith, spiritualism, festive fervor, traditions, conventions, customs; all these realities come in the way of their flight of fancy and ideological leaps. Essentially, they believe in what Fredrick Hayek called constructivism—that is, the belief that the society and the polity can be constructed as per a blue print.

It must be noted that secularism is proving to be a malaise not only in India but in the entire world. Secularists, with support from liberals and Left loonies, are determined to destroy all that is traditional, conventional, and of course religious. The attack on Christianity in the Western world is merely a manifestation of the spreading pandemic of secularism.

The purveyors of political correctness are burning midnight oil to banish the biggest Christian festival. In an article in *The Times* (London) before the Christmas of 2005, the Archbishop of Canterbury, Lord Carey of Clifton, rightly said that the public expression of the Christian faith and other religions was being undermined by political correctness. His views followed the decision of a Derbyshire school to send home a pupil for wearing a crucifix. There has also been criticism of some local authorities which renamed Christmas lights as "winter lights" to avoid offending other religions.

But are non-Christians offended? In response to the Archbishop's article, a letter to *The Times* by William McNeill, Elizabethtown, NC, USA, said, "Two friends of mine—one Jewish, the other Hindu—tell me how pleased they are to receive a Christmas card from me each year. Just this afternoon, my Jewish friend called and complained about attending her granddaughter's school's "Holiday" program, which consisted entirely of modern, secular, and predictably sappy holiday ditties. Not one traditional carol was included in the program. My friend was disappointed and angered by the school's politically correct zealots who would not allow any of the beautiful traditional religious carols to taint the program "because they might offend".

Another letter, by M. Nathan, London, said, "Lord Carey's comments regarding the undermining of Christianity in this Country are extremely welcome. As a Jew, and a proud one at that, I recognize the central importance and huge benefit of Christianity to our society. On the one hand it provides, through festivals such as Christmas, a national identity, one of the essential building blocks of that intangible thing oddly referred to as "Britishness". However it also is an essential component to maintaining religious

harmony. The fact that Christianity has been so dominant has ensured that the fights we witness throughout the world between religions seeking supremacy, are all but impossible here at home. That this dominance has started to be challenged, as Lord Carey highlights, is deeply troubling for our society."

Another letter, an angrier one, by John Smart from Telford, said, "How much longer are the vast majority of British people going to tolerate the sinister attempts by the politically correct brigade to undermine our Christian values and traditions? This is being done in the name of those who choose to live in this country, yet a Punjabi councilor was instrumental in restoring the Christmas message to the lights in Wolverhampton. He had consulted Sikhs, Hindus and Muslims asking if they were offended in any way by the traditions of Christmas. They responded with a unanimous "no". If they don't mind, who does, and what's more to the point, why are we letting it happen? The time has come for people to stand up against these politically-motivated bigots who profess to speak for minorities."

It's a pertinent question: if the minorities don't mind, who does? "Politically-motivated bigots" surely play their dirty games; but they are not the progenitors of such detestable campaigns; the real villains are intellectuals of various hues who want to mold the entire world as per their fancies and fantasies. They are the most intolerant and insolent of human beings; they can't tolerate the joys and raptures of ordinary people; they want the entire society to behave in a fashion that passes the test of "secular" and "progressive" culture. Hence the crusade against Christmas.

We must understand that such secular lunacy will not remain confined to the West; it is bound to reach India. Today, Christmas is under attack; tomorrow Diwali will be. Unless this secular madness is confronted in a robust manner, it will continue to spread like plague.

8 Mani Shankar Aiyar
Delicacies from Jurassic Park

Petroleum & Natural Gas Minister Mani Shankar Aiyar is an anachronism. He still loiters in the Nehruvian dreamscape of the 1950s and 1960s; and when he finds that the country and the world have moved on, he gets upset. But he is an honest man, in the sense that he lives his ideology: he is not a hypocrite. Unlike the Pritish Nandys, who inveigh against Hindu nationalism and then seek favors from the hated Hindu nationalists, Aiyar lives his ideology, howsoever rotten it may be.

And it is the rottenness of his ideology that more often than not makes his position untenable. In an article, "For Israel, A Gujarati View" (April 29, 2002) in *The Indian Express*, he wrote:

> Yasser Arafat's envoy to New Delhi has returned to Gaza City a deeply disillusioned man. The India of Jaswant Singh, he has discovered, is no longer the India of Nehru and Indira and Rajiv Gandhi. Jaswant Singh has had nothing constructive to offer, not even a heart-felt word of solace, in this the worst conjuncture for Palestine since The Catastrophe of 1948, the conquest of Palestine by Israeli terrorists, al-Naqba as it is called in the Arab world.
>
> Ariel Sharon is the Narendra Modi of Israel. Naroda Patiya is to Gujarat what Jenin is to Palestine. And just as Naroda Patiya is only the worst of a series of grisly atrocities deliberately inflicted

as an act of revenge on a hapless people, so is Jenin only the worst of a vicious vengeance exacted from blameless innocents. If the Muslim pogrom in Gujarat is justified as "action-reaction" for Godhra, so is Jenin exculpated as "action-reaction" for a suicide bombing at a Passover party. That those who are killed had nothing to do with those who were killed is regarded with as much nonchalance by the Tel Aviv government as by the government in Gandhinagar. And just as Sharon, the Butcher of Qibaya in 1948, and of Sabra and Shatila in 1982, is the same as the Butcher of Jenin, Bethlehem and Ramallah in 2002, so are the mass murderers in Gujarat of the same stock as those who assassinated Gandhiji in 1948, razed the masjid at Ayodhya in 1992, and undertook the genocide of Gujarat in 2002. And even as the Sharon of 2002 is no "aberration", so also, notwithstanding the pathetic cover-up by Jaswant Singh's ministry, is the Sangh Parivar of 2002 no "aberration". Jenin was written into the Likud victory in the Israel elections as clearly as Gujarat was written into the ascendance of the BJP in ours. The BJP is the Likud in saffron, as the Zionist Movement is the BJP in gaberdine (reference Shylock to Antonio in *The Merchant of Venice*: "You call me misbeliever, cut-throat dog / And spit upon my Jewish gaberdine").

Quite apart from the vituperative language, and rabid anti-Semitism, it is the mendacity of Aiyar that is unsettling. Israeli Prime Minister Ariel Sharon is "the Narendra Modi of Israel"—the harshest term in his arsenal. Further, Sharon is the "Butcher of Oibaya in 1948, and of Sabra and Shatila in 1982"; he is also the "Butcher of Jenin, Bethlehem and Ramalla in 2002". But not a word about Yasser Arafat, who spent his life as a terrorist, who organized a number of violent groups, whose actions were responsible for the murder of countless innocent men, women, and children. In Aiyar's scheme of things, Arafat is a "freedom fighter"; if so, are all those who proclaim to fight for "freedom" ethically or legally permitted to carry out terrorism!

Ion Mihai Pacepa, the senior most official of communist Romania who defected to the US, has a different story to tell. In an

article on Arafat in the *Wall Street Journal* (January 12, 2002), he wrote:

> The 72-year-old Palestinian leader . . . is a career terrorist, trained, armed and bankrolled by the Soviet Union and its satellites for decades.
>
> Before I defected to America from Romania, leaving my post as chief of Romanian intelligence, I was responsible for giving Arafat about $200,000 in laundered cash every month throughout the 1970s. I also sent two cargo planes to Beirut a week, stuffed with uniforms and supplies. Other Soviet bloc states did much the same. Terrorism has been extremely profitable for Arafat. According to *Forbes* magazine, he is today the sixth wealthiest among the world's "kings, queens & despots", with more than $300 million stashed in Swiss bank accounts.
>
> "I invented the hijackings [of passenger planes]," Arafat bragged when I first met him at his PLO headquarters in Beirut in the early 1970s . . . . The dubious honor of inventing hijacking actually goes to the KGB, which first hijacked a U.S. passenger plane in 1960 to Communist Cuba. Arafat's innovation was the suicide bomber, a terror concept that would come to full flower on 9/11 . . . .
>
> I was given the KGB's "personal file" on Arafat. He was an Egyptian bourgeois turned into a devoted Marxist by KGB foreign intelligence. The KGB had trained him at its Balashikha special-ops school east of Moscow and in the mid-1960s decided to groom him as the future PLO leader. First, the KGB destroyed the official records of Arafat's birth in Cairo, replacing them with fictitious documents saying that he had been born in Jerusalem and was therefore a Palestinian by birth . . . .
>
> . . . the KGB gave Arafat an ideology and an image, just as it did for loyal Communists in our international front organizations. High-minded idealism held no mass-appeal in the Arab world, so the KGB remolded Arafat as a rabid anti-Zionist. They also selected a "personal hero" for him—the Grand Mufti Haj Amin al-Husseini, the man who visited Auschwitz in the late 1930s and reproached the Germans for not having killed even more Jews. In

> 1985 Arafat paid homage to the mufti, saying he was "proud no end" to be walking in his footsteps.

So much for Aiyar's freedom fighter. But Aiyar does not stop here. In his scheme of things, the death of 1,000 people in Gujarat is "genocide"; but the killings of Hindus in Bangladesh, presumably, are an "internal matter" of our neighboring state! I don't remember him—or, for that matter, any other liberal—crying, raving, and ranting about the plight of Hindus in Bangladesh. This despite the fact the number of non-Muslims has seen a continuous decline in that country since Partition—from almost one-third of the population to below 10 per cent.

Aiyar's ideology is not shaken by such empirical evidence of ethnic cleansing. The fulmination continues, so do falsehoods:

> Faced with human tragedy of this magnitude [that is, violence at Jenin], Jaswant Singh can go no further in asking Sharon to desist than Vajpayee can restrain Narendra Modi. For even as Vajpayee admires Modi for being a better Rashtriya Swayam Sewak than his NDA-compromised self, so does Jaswant Singh profoundly believe that the Israeli way is the right way. That mindset was exposed when our external affairs minister—in Jerusalem, of all places—attributed our decades-long Palestine policy to the "Muslim votebank". Unable to believe that even a BJP external affairs minister could be so irresponsible, I asked for confirmation from the external publicity division and was informed that the minister had indeed said exactly that. I gave Jaswant Singh the opportunity to retract or apologize on the floor of the House; the offer was haughtily refused. The saffron beast behind the ex-major's suave countenance was never more nakedly revealed. The BJP believes in its bones that there is nothing more than the "Muslim votebank" to Gandhi declaring in the twenties [1920s] that "Palestine belongs to the Palestinians as England belongs to the English and France to the French"; to the 1947 Nehru formula of a federal state of Israel/Palestine; and to the half-century of unflinching Indian solidarity with the mercilessly

> persecuted Palestinians which preceded the advent of the BJP to power in our benighted land.

But, Mr. Aiyar, what is "so irresponsible" in accepting a truth and stating it in plain words? Wasn't it the consideration of Muslim vote-bank that prodded Congress regimes support a terrorist like Arafat? Wasn't it because of the Muslim vote-bank that, till P.V. Narasimha Rao took the courageous step of normalizing relations with Israel, India blindly backed the Arabs at all international forums? This despite the fact that many Arab nations supported Pakistan and aided fundamentalist bodies in India. In fact, we proved to be more Arab than Arabs, for even when many Arab nations normalized relations with Israel, we refused to do so. As for Mahatma Gandhi's stand on Palestine, we must remember that his was not the last word on international affairs (for that matter, his was not the last word even on national issues, and for this reason Aiyar's god, Nehru, often ignored Gandhi's advice, even on a matter so close to Gandhi's heart as India's partition!). To cite just one example, Gandhi had once advised the German Jews to willingly submit to Hitler and wait for his change of heart! This was Gandhian wisdom on foreign affairs. And as for Nehru and his formulas, he was the founder-promoter of the Muslim vote-bank. But Aiyar does not wish to recognize this fact. In another article, he wrote: "Nehru won [the 1952 general election] because he did not flinch. He refused—adamantly—to let considerations of vote-bank politics sway his resolve."

It is not only when Aiyar is discussing politics that he presents twisted facts and mutilated truths; he does the same when he discusses economics. In an article, "Sinha vs Singh", in *The Indian Express* (March 5, 2002), he wrote:

> GDP growth during Manmohan's four years was steadily raised from 5.1 per cent to 7.5 per cent. Indeed, the momentum imparted to growth took us to over 8 per cent the following year. It has been a downslide ever since. Yashwant's record is a slithering from 6.4 per cent in 1998-99 to 5.4 per cent in 2001-02, after touching a low of 3.9 per cent in 2000-01. Indeed, the terminal

> figure is something of a statistical illusion given the low growth in the previous year as the average for the two years combined amounts to only 4.6 per cent. Yet, in every budget speech, Sinha pulls out the magic figure of plus seven per cent annual growth as the road to India's economic heaven. When Manmohan did the same, it made sense as we were actually on a plus 7 per cent growth path. To repeat the same mantra when one is down to a 4-5 per cent trajectory is to think you can fool all of the people all of the time. The fact is we were within reach of the Asian economic miracle under Manmohan Singh; we are now tottering on the brink of a reversal to the notorious "Hindu" rate of growth.

This is just partisan argumentation. Aiyar presents the scenario as good and competent Manmohan Singh versus bad and incompetent Yashwant Sinha. The truth is that both are politicians of indifferent variety, in whose scheme of things expedience precedes conviction. In fact, Aiyar is better than both of them because he sticks to his principles. On the other hand, there is nothing that can be called Singh vs Sinha; both are the two faces of the same coin, the coin called careerism. Singh was a socialist when socialism was in fashion; he demolished it when he, and his masters, found it expedient. Sinha served the socialist Prime Minister Chandra Shekhar with as much bureaucratic coldness as he served the allegedly Rightwing Atal Bihari Vajpayee.

But sometimes, Aiyar goes beyond partisan argumentation, and makes observations that are untenable. In an article, "Growth, But It's Jobless," in *The Indian Express* (December 23, 2003), he wrote:

> Neither privatization nor globalization appears to be the magic answer, because employment in the organized private sector (domestic and multinational) is currently growing at a minuscule 0.1 per cent per annum. So says the government's latest Economic Survey. Moreover, the 1993-2000 employment survey also says that *notional* job loss—that is, job loss on account of the slowing of employment growth rates—is running at nearly 84 lakh a year. If we are losing jobs at the rate of 84 lakh per year,

> *where is the prime minister discovering a net addition of 84 lakh a year*? [emphasis added]

Notice the ruse of transforming *notional* into *real*. Had 84 lakh people lost jobs every year during the 1993-2000 period, the consequences would have been calamitous for the nation; there would have countrywide demonstrations and social unrest; prosperity would not have been so widespread and visible in the 1990s as it was.

Aiyar is right in saying that job growth in the organized sector during 1993-2000 was minuscule, but it's people of his persuasion who are responsible for this sorry state of affairs. It was the Left-libbers like Aiyar who helped create a business environment that frowns upon entrepreneurship, discourages endeavor, and penalizes success. Nehru believed that capitalism, if not regulated, would make the rich richer and the poor poorer. He and his progeny—Aiyar is definitely Nehru's ideological progeny—chained the economy so tightly and so badly that even more than a decade of liberalization has failed to completely unshackle it. If a large number of investors are not attracted to India and not many jobs are coming up, as Aiyar complains, it is because of the mindless rules and regulations created and imposed on the economy by his ideological brethren in the heyday of Congress rule. Be it roads, ports, airports, airlines, Railways, the power sector, or the labor regime—the depredations of socialism are everywhere, and for everybody to see. Provided, of course, they want to see such depredations.

But then Aiyar does not *want* to see the complete failure of socialism in India, or elsewhere. He also does not want to see many other things. Let's see what he has to say about Pakistan. In another article, "Negotiating in Good Faith," in *The Indian Express* (January 22, 2002), he wrote:

> Diplomatic maturity demands that we recognize that there are Pakistani perceptions and Pakistani concerns and that we cannot expect Pakistan to mouth the Indian line any more than Pakistan can expect India to mouth the Pakistani line.

But what are "Pakistani perceptions and Pakistani concerns" other than exporting Islamic terror to Kashmir and other parts of India? And why does Aiyar bracket India with Pakistan? India is a democracy, with a decent Constitution, democratic institutions, and a vibrant civil society; Pakistan is a theocracy, run by a deceitful general, a country that is gradually accepting the rigid Shariat laws and whose society is dominated by fundamentalist mullahs. After a little exercise in moral equivalence, Aiyar starts sermonizing:

> A dialogue is required precisely because of our differences. And a dialogue is most required when the situation is at its most tense. Moreover, because our differences run so deep and wide, time and patience—but, above all, goodwill and good faith—are required to fill the gap. We do not know where the dialogue will lead and how long it will take. For if we did, there would be no need for dialogue, we could go directly to the answers. So, let us expect the opening Pakistani position to be as hard as ours. Then let us try to understand each other and persuade each other. And out of such mutual understanding, Inshallah, reconciliation, or at least accommodation, might prove possible. But strong-arm negotiating tactics, bullying, bluster and posturing will lead nowhere—other than to the UN Security Council resolution of June 1998.

So, a dialogue with Pakistan "is most required". It sends terrorists to India, but we should we should start dialogue, build "goodwill and good faith" between the two nations! Had Aiyar been speaking about the "strong-arm negotiating tactics, bullying, bluster and posturing" by Pakistan, it would have made some sense; but he is again speaking about both countries, which effectively again puts them on an equal footing; that is, he is equating the villain with the victim. If Aiyar were India's Prime Minister or foreign minister, our government would meekly accept the Islamic terrorists sent by Pakistan, offering them the entire country to do whatever they wanted to. We would wait till the murderers and rapists, sadists and torturers undergo a Gandhian change of heart.

They would organize massacres; our security personnel would look the other way. Pakistan would continue its bloody games; India would build "goodwill and faith". That all this is no hyperbole becomes evident from Aiyar's statement in Parliament (on December 22, 2003) where he reverently quoted Gandiji: "Forgiveness is more manly than punishment. Forgiveness adorns a soldier"; "If India takes up the doctrine of the sword, she may gain momentary victory but then it will cease to be the prize of my heart." In his article, too, Aiyar makes it amply clear that he has great faith in Gandhi: "We cannot bully Pakistan out of anything. But we can persuade them of a great deal—provided we ourselves are reasonable and as prepared to listen as to hector. Our model should be the greatest Indian negotiator of them all—Mohandas Karamchand Gandhi."

Even a cursory familiarity with history would reveal that Gandhi himself was unable to "persuade" Jinnah to abandon his demand for Pakistan. And, surely, Aiyar knows his history. Yet, he persists in his blinkered views.

Aiyar reiterates his penchant for pacifist folly in another article:

> There is no military solution to terrorism, domestic or cross-border. Root causes require political treatment, diplomatic treatment. State violence can only be an adjunct to non-violent action. For, above all, as Mahatma Gandhi cautioned us in 1934: "We must have more faith in our non-violence than the terrorist has in his violence."

So, keep up the flag of non-violence, whatever the consequences, harangues Aiyar. He refuses to see, despite a mountain of evidence and cogent arguments, that Gandhi's is a failed philosophy; that evil does exist and can only be eliminated by using force; that the threat of Islamic terror is real; that political problems deserve political treatment and terrorism is not a political problem; terrorism is a law and order problem. Given a chance, Aiyar would adorn every soldier, cop, prosecutor, and magistrate with forgiveness; all of them would join the Don Quixotes of India to build "goodwill and good faith".

According to Aiyar, "Either Gandhi was a fraud or his values are eternal." Such a line of thinking precludes rational understanding of the affairs of the world, for it does away with critical appraisal. If Gandhi's values are *not* eternal, it does *not* make him a crook. All of us come across people who are honest and simple, but their values may or may not be eternal. Are all such people frauds? Further, Gandhi may still be a great man, even if some of his ideas and views are crude. For instance, Gandhi called Parliament a "prostitute". So, should one deduce that he was a fascist?

The problem with Aiyar is that his understanding of politics, economy, and society is stupid, with little connectivity with the real world. He ardently believes in the absurdities taught in our universities, the most conspicuous of them being the distinctions between the Left and the Right. In an article, "Enron Educates India" in *The Indian Express* (December 11, 2001), he wrote:

> The Indian right has such a divine faith in the market that their most articulate ideologue could find nothing but praise for the market having punished Enron for their cupidity much quicker and more effectively than the long arm of the law could have done. Thus Enron's crookedness is also invoked to justify our transition out of stodgy socialism. What the right wing forgets is that while it is of little consequence to us as Indians whether the small American investor, who put his savings and faith in the booming stock of Enron and its multifarious ventures, was cheated or not, it does matter to us enormously as Indians that Enron were flouting American law. For does that not also indicate that they were up to nefarious sharp practice in India as well?

This is unadulterated pedantry. The Left, we are taught, is anti-capitalism, pro-poor, secular, etc; the Right, on the other hand, is pro-capitalism, anti-poor, fascist, etc. Aiyar blindly accepts such classifications and applies them to the real world. Had he bothered to just look around, he would have noticed that what he calls "the Indian right" actually works against the spirit, tenets, and ideals of capitalism. The Sangh Parivar, which Aiyar calls the Indian right,

has played a greater role in slowing down the rollback of socialism than his party, the Congress, and even the communists have. It is mainly because of the pressure of the Parivar that the privatization drive came to a grinding halt in the middle of 2002; the Parivar is opposed to the raising of cap on foreign direct investment in any sector; it is also against the removal of various subsidies; it wants the role of the state to increase in many sectors, particularly education and health. Yet, Aiyar talks about the Indian Right's "divine faith in the market".

Aiyar sounds most irrational, ludicrous, and outlandish when he talks US affairs. In an article, "Stand Up, Be Counted," in *The Indian Express* (November 5, 2001), he wrote:

> Now that George W. Bush's bombing of Afghanistan is proving the flop show of the millennium, is it not time India injected some good sense into the so-called global war against terrorism?

Flop show! Within three months of the WTC attacks, America was in a position to oust the barbaric regime in Kabul, and Aiyar finds it a flop show! But he continues the delicacies from Jurassic Park:

> Non-alignment was the extension into foreign policy of the principles that informed our freedom movement. Yet, the fierce independence of mind and spirit which once so characterized us as a nation is nowhere to be seen as we hobble behind others hoping our presence in the queue will be recognized. At the Non-aligned Summit in New Delhi in 1983, Indira Gandhi described the non-aligned movement as "the biggest peace movement in the world". Today, we are embarrassed to talk about peace for fear it might mute the thumping of our chests.

The fact is that the non-alignment movement (NAM) never made significant impact on global affairs. The West never considered it more than a minor irritant; for the Soviet Union, the movement was little more than a front organization where it could garner support from scores of nations, all chanting the slogans against imperialism and neo-imperialism—like the sheep in Or-

well's *Animal Farm.* India showed some commonsense in downsizing its zeal for this sham movement, though a quick burial would have been a better idea.

But Aiyar's heart still beat for the supposedly glorious past of NAM, when at loud jamborees some of the worst tyrants lambasted the West for its real and largely imaginary sins:

> In 1989, Rajiv Gandhi wrote a hundred-page letter to Gorbachev—at Gorbachev's request—explaining how insurrection against the state cannot be met by violence alone and how the Indian experience of tackling terrorism showed that it was only through dialogue, accommodation and reconciliation that the root causes of terrorism can be contained. Now when Vajpayee gets a call from Bush, one can hear the strains of the Stars and Stripes being played in the PMO as background music.

Now, criticizing the country's Prime Minister is one thing, presenting him as an obsequies lackey is in bad taste. Besides, one wonders if Gorbachev ever took of Rajiv Gandhi's advice, or that of any other Indian leader, with any seriousness. In any case, what sensible advice could poor Rajiv have rendered when his own advisers were of Aiyar's ilk?

The funniest part of Aiyar's twaddle is that he believes in it. According to him, "We lost our moral leadership of the non-aligned movement when we went nuclear." But did we ever enjoy any leadership—moral, political, economic, or military? What morality was involved in allying with some of the worst tyrants in the high noon of Thirdworldism? What morality was involved in supporting bellicose Arab states against Israel? Why was India responsible for the vivisection of Pakistan? Why did we intervene in Sri Lanka without exhausting the option of UN, about whose global role we pontificate so passionately? Why is Aiyar so hard-bent on deceiving others and himself? And why does he blame everything on the West?

But Aiyar continues:

> If the Anglo-American combine had not so foolishly overthrown Mossadeq, not just Iran but much of West Asia would have pro-

> gressed to modern and prosperous democracy. If France and the United Kingdom had not invaded Egypt in 1956, they might have counted for something more than poodles. Similarly, if the West had not egged on Saddam Hussein to invade Ayatollah Khomeini's Iran, he would not have felt able to barge into Kuwait with impunity.

Blaming everything on others, especially the West, is the hallmark of Leftist ideology, which is blindly followed by the liberals such as Aiyar and Muslim intellectuals like Rafiq Zakaria and Mushirul Hasan. The result is self-deception and wishful thinking: "Perhaps there is a Third World Nehru somewhere out there who will take up the baton which Jaswant Singh has dropped with such a clang."

Wishful, from Aiyar's point of view. We pray that such wishes are never fulfilled.

9 Islam's Marriage with Terrorism

One would have expected intellectuals and liberals to strongly oppose the rigidities, obscurantism, bigotry, and dogmatism of Islam; indeed to raise basic question about a faith which has not seen any reforms and which is at odds with the rest of the world that has moved towards modernity, rationalism, and humanism. Liberals and intellectuals should have critically examined Islam; on the contrary, all over the world they use all the sophistry and chicanery they can muster to shield Islam from any critical scrutiny; they end up as apologists for the growing Islamist militancy. To defend the indefensible, they generate spurious doctrines, such as that of multiculturalism, moral relativism, and composite culture.

Leftwing intellectuals and liberals unquestionably go along with the claim that Islam is a religion of peace that it stands for fraternity and equality. As for violence associated with Islam, they argue that the terrorists distort the "real meaning" of Islam, thus maligning the great faith. The great faith, assert liberals, further suffers at the hands of the media. The media—Western as well as Indian—depicts the Muslims as fanatics and Islam as a violent religion. This is how Islam and Muslims are "stereotyped". Or so the Leftist and the liberal claim.

As on other issues, Indian intellectuals are loath to see the reality as it exists. They continue to ignore facts and twist truths. They continue to confuse myth-making with scholarship, and propa-

ganda with perspicacity. They make great effort to veil the many passages in the *Koran* that explicitly instruct the faithful to slay non-Muslims, wage jihad, ill-treat women, and straitjacket life into prescription. These are the passages that have always inspired, and continue to inspire, violent men in the community to live up to the exhortations and instructions.

It is true that the vast majority of Muslims are peace-loving people; what is tragic is that the small, violent minority is able to impose its fundamentalist agenda on the majority without much protest from the latter. And intellectuals continue to pussy-foot around this reality.

Let's us scrutinize some of the falsehoods about Islam which liberals spread. Inherently, there is nothing in the precepts and tenets of Islam that can inspire terrorist activities, for essentially it is a peaceful religion, implore our intellectuals. It is a lunatic fringe in the Muslim community—and, mind you, such a fringe exists in every community, be it Hindu, Christian, Sikh, or Jew—that is at the root of all problems. And one should never forget the "root-cause", say the champions of liberalism. The root-cause is always "socio-economic" conditions, and such conditions inevitably generate terrorism and violence. It is not Islam but poverty and political alienation that are root-cause (Liberals conveniently stop at socio-economic conditions, not looking for the *root-cause of* adverse socio-economic conditions. But let that pass).

They also quote selectively from the *Koran* to buttress their arguments: "There shall be no compulsion in religion" (Sura 2:256). Conveniently, they do not quote other suras of the *Koran*, those preach violence and intolerance.

"Our Marxist professors and other pundits of Secularism are very much mistaken when they discover or invent economic and/or political motives for explaining away the crimes committed by Islam," writes Sita Ram Goel in his momentous *Hindu Temples: What Happened to Them*. He goes on to substantiate his claim. What Goel did was pack his work primarily with the extracts and evidence from contemporary historians. But we shall

begin with Islam's record, as detailed in another authoritative account.

It is a bestselling book, *Islam Unveiled: Disturbing Questions About the World's Fastest Growing Faith*, by Robert Spencer. Spencer, the director of Jihad Watch, is a writer and researcher who has written six books, seven monographs, and well over a hundred articles about jihad and Islamic terrorism. His latest book is the *New York Times* bestseller *The Politically Incorrect Guide to Islam (and the Crusades)* (Regnery). He is coauthor, with Daniel Ali, of *Inside Islam: A Guide for Catholics* (Ascension), and editor of the essay collection *The Myth of Islamic Tolerance: How Islamic Law Treats Non-Muslims* (Prometheus). His next book, *The Truth About Muhammad*, is coming October 9 from Regnery Publishing. Spencer (MA, Religious Studies, University of North Carolina at Chapel Hill) has been studying Islamic theology, law, and history in depth since 1980. He is an Adjunct Fellow with the Free Congress Foundation.

His articles on Islam and other topics have appeared in the *New York Post*, the *Washington Times*, the *Dallas Morning News*, Canada's *National Post*, *FrontPage Magazine.com*, *WorldNet Daily*, *Insight in the News*, *Human Events*, *National Review Online*, and many other journals. He has consulted with United States Central Command on Islam and jihad, and has discussed jihad, Islam, and terrorism at a workshop sponsored by the U.S. State Department and the German Foreign Ministry, as well as on the BBC, CNN, FoxNews, MSNBC, PBS, C-Span, and Croatia National Television (HTV), as well as on numerous radio programs.

In his book, *Islam Unveiled*, Robert Spencer has described in detail how *jaziya*, the poll tax non-Muslims have to pay under Muslim rule, was collected: "The *jaziya* had to be paid in public, in a bizarre and degrading ceremony that required the Muslim tax official to hit the *dhimmi* [the non-Muslim subject] on the head or the back of the neck. This ritualized violence symbolized, of course, the subjugation of the *dhimmis*. The twelfth century

Qur'anic commentator Zamakhshari, in fact, directed that the *jaziya* should be collected 'with belittlement and humiliation'."

Whether it were the Christians in the Ottomon Empire and the Arab world, the Hindus in India, or the Bahais in Persia, the kafirs suffered the same fate under any Muslim ruler. Muslim rule in the Ottomon Empire, writes Spencer, "led to a blizzard of laws regulating clothing for Christians and Jews, and in some places Christians even had to wear a sort of modified tonsure by shaving the fronts of the heads."

Further, "often the Muslim authorities buttressed these laws with others that restricted or denied altogether the *dhimmis'* access to public baths and other public spaces. In some places, Christians and Jews could go to the baths, but only they wore small bells on their fingers and toes so that, even when unclothed, they could be identified and duly shunned . . . . Other laws assigned distasteful duties to the *dhimmis*, such as removal of dead animals and the cleaning of public toilets."

According to Spencer:

> The effects of such laws were manifold. A *dhimmi* could never blend into the crowd. He had to keep to the side of the street and could not be greeted the way ordinary people were greeted; he was an inferior, and unclean. These wretched fellows could become a target for Muslim anytime, anywhere. After all, the principle behind these laws was that anyone who remained a Jew or a Christian in a Muslim milieu must be deliberately perverse, with a heart so set against Allah as to refuse to acknowledge the manifest truth and superiority of Islam. Such people were natural targets for popular resentment, and the *dhimmis* often were subject to random violence.

Even Philip Hitti, a celebrated scholar of Islam who was also quite sympathetic to it, wrote about Ottomon rule: "The Caliph al-Mutawakkil in 850 and 854 decreed that Christians and Jews should affix wooden images of devils to their houses, level their graves even with the ground, wear outer garments of honey color, i.e. yellow, put tow honey-colored patches on the clothes of their

slaves . . . and ride only on mules and asses with wooden saddles marked by two pomegranate-like balls on the cantle."

Things were no better in India. In his book on Hindu temples, Sita Ram Goel has presented indisputable evidence to expose the lie of Leftist historian Satish Chandra that Muslim rulers followed a "policy of broad toleration". Goel has quoted all the important historians of the period—Barani, Sirajud-din, Ferishta, Abdullah Sirhindi, etc. Goel has also quoted Sultan Firuz Shah Tughlaq himself who boasted of destroying temples and killing "leaders of infidelity"— all this, of course, "under divine guidance" and in accordance with "the Law of the Prophet which declared that such temples are not to be tolerated". Furthermore, "I also ordered that the infidel books, the idols, and the vessels used in their worship, which had been taken with them, should all be publicly burnt." The same Sultan is also lauded for breaking the idols of Nagarkot in Himachal Pradesh, "mixing the fragments [of idols] with pieces of cow's flesh," filling bags with them, and tying the bags around the necks of Brahmins, "who were then paraded through the camp."

Ferishta wrote about Sultan Ahmad Shah I Wali Bahmani (1422-35):

> Ahmud Shah, without waiting to besiege the Hindoo capital, overran the open country; and wherever he went put to death men, women, and children, without mercy, contrary to the compact made between uncle and predecessor, Mahomed Shah, and the Rays of Beejanuggar [Vijayanagar]. Whenever the number of slain amounted to twenty thousand, he halted three days, and a made a festival celebration of the bloody event. He broke down, also, the idolatrous temples, and destroyed the colleges of Brahmins . . .

According to Goel:

> Starting with Al-Biladhuri who wrote in Arabic in the second half of the ninth century, and coming down to Syed Mahmudul Hasan who wrote in English in the fourth decade of the twentieth, we have cited from *eighty* histories spanning a period of more than *twelve hundred years*. Our citations mention *sixty-one*

> kings, *sixty-three* military commanders and *fourteen* Sufis who destroyed Hindu temples in *one hundred and fifty-four* localities, big and small, spread from Khurasan in the West to Tripura in the East, and from Transoxiana in the North to Tamil Nadu in the South, over a period of *eleven hundred years* . . . Allah was thanked every time for enabling the iconoclast concerned to render service to the religion of Muhammad by means of this pious performance.

The vandalism, massacres, and pillage were not only recorded by the contemporary chroniclers but the perpetrators "took immense pride in doing what they did". Goel concludes:

> It is inconceivable that a constant and consistent behavior pattern, witnessed for a long time and over a vast area, can be explained except in terms of a settled system of belief which leaves no scope for second thoughts. Looking at the very large number of temples, big and small, destroyed or desecrated or converted into Muslim monuments, economic or political explanations can be only a futile, if not fraudulent, exercise. The explanations are not even plausible.

Yet, historian after Leftwing historian has worked tirelessly to provide economic or political explanations to Muslim depredations; they have tried to explain away such depredations. And our liberal intellectuals hail Leftwing histories as examples of great scholarship! Sita Ram Goel is, without doubt, an abominable knickerwallah, an odious rabble-rouser. It is another matter that no Marxist historian or liberal intellectual has been able to refute the evidence provided by Goel; nor has anybody countered any of his arguments. So the Left-liberal mafia adopts its favorite tactic—denial without arguments; just denounce the enemy as vile, without citing any example of his vileness, and keep on denouncing him *ad nauseum.* Till his vileness becomes an axiomatic truth, an accepted postulate in public discourse. A relentless recourse to *argumentum ad hominem.*

When speaking the truth becomes a dangerous venture, mendacity attracts a premium. Mendacity catches the attention of the

merchant bankers of public discourse—academics, authors, and senior journalists. Nowadays the merchants of mendacity are busy selling Islam, packaged as "a peaceful religion".

Let's begin with the *Koran* itself, the most authentic text of Islam in the eyes of Muslims, it being the Word of Allah. What does the *Koran* say about kafirs, or unbelievers? "They are the worst of creatures" (*Koran*, 98.6). Sura 8 goes even farther, denouncing unbelievers of misguiding and killing the faithful: "Remember how the Unbelievers plotted against thee, to keep thee in bonds, or slay thee, to get thee out (of thy homes). They plot and plan, and Allah too plans; but the best of planners is Allah." (8:30)

Again, "The Unbelievers spend their wealth to hinder (men) from the path of Allah, and so will they continue to spend; but in the end they will have (only) regrets and sighs; at length they will be overcome; and the Unbelievers will be gathered together to Hell." (8:36)

And again, "Say to the Unbelievers, if (now) they desist (from Unbelief), their past would be forgiven them; but if they persist, the punishment of those before them is already (a matter of warning for them). (8:38)

The *Koran* reminds and exhorts: "Remember the Lord inspired the angels (with the message): 'I am with you: give firmness to the Believers: I will instill terror into the hearts of the Unbelievers; smite ye above their necks and smite all their fingertips off them'." (8:12)

One can go on and on, citing sura after sura about the intolerance of Islam as reflected in the *Koran* and in the *Hadees*. Exhortations from the *Koran* and the *Hadees* have always prodded not only the Caliphs and Sultans to massacre and plunder but also inspired men of letters to glorify the exploits of murderers. Amir Khusru was one of them. A symbol of composite culture—which is the *desi* term for multiculturalism—the thirteenth-fourteenth century scholar was a historian, poet, musician, and a man of wide interests. But he was also, as Sita Ram Goel rightfully describes him, "the lick-spittle of whoever came out victorious in the contest for the throne at Delhi"—a trait common in many intellectuals of

contemporary India as well. According to Goel, "Amir Khusru describes with great glee how the heads of Brahmans 'danced from their necks and fell to the ground at their feet', along with those of the other 'infidels' whom Malik Kafur had slaughtered during the sack of the temples at Chidambaram."

Goel has also quoted passages from Khusru, allegedly a great icon of Hindu-Muslim amity. "When the royal army [of Alau'din Khalji] reached that province [Gujarat], it won a victory after great slaughter . . . The army of Islam broke the idols [at Somnath] and the biggest idol was sent to the court of the Sultan." This is Khusru—the icon of inter-religious faith! Goel wonders "whether the poet of Islam is being honored or slandered when he is presented in our own times as the pioneer of Secularism."

It gave great joy to Khusru to see the Islamic conquest of Deccan and south India: "The tongue of the sword of the Khalifa of the time, which is the tongue of the flame of Islam, has imparted light to the entire darkness of Hindustan by the illumination of its guidance . . . the army has conquered from sea to sea, and several capitals of the gods of the Hindus in which Satanism had prevailed since the time of the Jinns, have been demolished. All these impurities of infidelity have been cleansed by the Sultan's destruction of idol temples, beginning with his first expedition against Deogir, so that the flames of the light of the law illuminate all these unholy countries, and places for the cries to prayers are exalted on high, and prayers are read in mosques. God be praised!" So much for composite culture and communal harmony.

But liberals and intellectuals argue that there is no point in getting obsessed with the past; let's concentrate on the present, they say. The focus should be on promoting harmony between various religions, rather than on raking up the conflicts of the past.

So, let's concentrate on the current situation. Today, terrorism has become synonymous with Islam: the terror of Islam haunts the entire world. Be it New York or Tel Aviv, Bombay or Bali—wherever there is terrorism, the signature of Islam is inevitable. This is no "stereotyping" by the media; this is no "Orientalism"; this is a fact. Liberal apologists for Islam argue that the LTTE is

involved in terrorist activities in Sri Lanka; many Sikhs fought a violent battle for Khalistan in the 1980s and the 1990s; there are armed militias in America; there are any number of fierce outfits in various parts in the world; but that does not mean that Hinduism (since LTTE is presumably Hindu), Sikhism, Christianity, etc, promote terrorism. Besides, the argument goes, Christians have fought crusades and Hindus have oppressed the lower castes; Islam, liberals say, is not unique in its imperfections.

It is true that followers of other religions are also involved in terrorist activities, but what is conspicuous is the preponderance of Muslims in terrorist activities. Further, as we saw earlier in this chapter, Islam explicitly and unequivocally exhorts its followers to indulge in violent activities against kafirs. Thus, the Islamist terrorist can find moral sanction in the teachings of Islam—and liberals and intellectuals are unwilling to accept this fact. As for the misdeeds of the followers of other religions in the past, they have evolved with time. The Christianity of the twenty first century is different from the Christianity of the eleventh century; ditto with Hinduism, Judaism, Buddhism, etc; but in Islam there has been little evolution. Even today, Muslims in substantial numbers believe in, and wage, jihad; attempts are made in different parts of the world to impose Shariat; the teaching of science is opposed in Muslim societies; freedom of artists and writers is frowned upon, and severely restricted, in Muslim countries; women are still stoned to death for adultery.

In fact, the manner in which women are treated in Muslim societies is, to put it mildly, appalling. There is no point in listing the barbaric laws, rules, and regulations in Muslim nations that restrict the freedom of women; efforts are made being to implement the practices recommended by Shariat such as stoning of adulteresses. Such efforts increased in scope in the 1970s, 1980s, and 1990s. Muslim women were freer in the 1960s than they are in the twenty first century—which is reverse of the trend in non-Muslim societies.

And again, it is the cardinal principles and essential tenets of Islam that are use to justify the plight of women. Liberals never tire

of pointing out the "egalitarian ethic" of Islam, of saying that Islam stipulated women's rights. They quote from the *Koran* which says that "women shall have rights similar to the rights against them, according to what is equitable". They, however, forget—or choose to overlook—the rider that the *Koran* immediately adds to such radical-sounding assertion. The full sentence is: "And women shall have rights similar to the rights against them, according to what is equitable; *but men have a degree (of advantage) over them.* And Allah is Exalted in Power, Wise" (2:228) [emphasis added]

Sura 4, An-Nisa, of the *Koran*, makes male dominance explicit, giving a short shrift to egalitarianism, at least between the genders:

> "Men are the managers of the affairs of women for that Allah has preferred in bounty one of them over another, and for that they have expended of their property. Righteous women are therefore obedient, guarding the secret for Allah's guarding. And those you fear may be rebellious, admonish them; banish them to their couches; and beat them. If they then obey you, look not for any way against them; Allah is All-high, All-great."

Since the *Koran* is the Word of Allah, this is the command of Allah. As a natural corollary, Prophet Mohammad (from Hadees) leaves no doubt whatsoever about the position of women in a Muslim society:

> When a man calls his wife to satisfy his desire, she must go to him even if she is occupied at the oven.
>
> If I were to command anyone to make prostration before another, I would command women to prostrate themselves before their husbands, because of the special right over them given to the husbands by Allah.
>
> A man will not be asked about why he beat his wife.
>
> If he [a husband] were to order her [his wife] to convey stones from a yellow mountain to a black one, or from a black mountain to a white one, it would be incumbent on her to do so.
>
> If a woman dies in a state when her husband is pleased with her, she will enter paradise.

There is no equivocation, either in the commands of Allah or in the Prophet's mind. There is no lack of clarity as to how Islam prescribes the treatment of women: they are undeniably inferior to men. As the greatest Muslim theologian Al-Ghazzali informed the faithful: "Merit has one thousand components, only one of which is attributable to women, while nine hundred ninety-nine are attributable to men."

So, when we see the plight of Muslim women all over the world, it is not—as liberals would have us believe—because of the "distortion of Islam by the obscurantist mullahs," or because of certain "socio-economic conditions"; it is because the scriptures prescribe the subjugation of women. Clearly, egalitarianism of Islam is phony—not only because half of mankind is simply doomed under it, but also because it accepts the practices such as slavery without any question.

One of the most important reasons for Islam's intolerance and narrow-mindedness is that its most important text, the *Koran*, is both *absolutely infallible* and *unalterable*, for it is the Word of Allah. Exegesis is ruled out, though heroic attempts have been made to reconcile the medieval faith with modern ethos—modernization of Turkey under Mustapha Kamal Ataturk, the Aligarh movement under Sir Syed Ahmad Khan, and Arab nationalism of Gamal Abdel Nasser being some of the most important ones. There was some limited success in Turkey, but here too it is the army's commitment to Ataturk's ideals guided it through. As late as in the 1990s an Islamist became Turkey's Prime Minister, though his regime was short-lived. Aligarh proved to be the breeding ground for militant Islam. And Arab nationalism degenerated into Saddam Hussein-like dictatorships.

The more important reason—perhaps *the most important reason*—is that Islam is transcendental totalitarianism. This is also the reason that it has survived for fourteen centuries while other forms of totalitarianism arose and failed in the twentieth century itself. It offers a *modus vivendi* that is holistic. The world of Islam may be small but it is consistent within itself; its theology jells with its mythology, politics, and sociology; it's a complete whole, com-

plete within itself. Islam is unlike communism, as it offers an otherworldly *summom bonum* to human existence: the Paradise is also an erotic universe in which all men would be provided houris and such carnal delights that the most libertine can only imagine of (typically, no such pleasures are reserved for good women, who are doomed even in paradise to compete with houris to attract the attention of their husbands!).

Islam is also different from other forms of totalitarianism, as it seeks to exercise *total* control over *all* human activities. Under communism and fascism, the state crushes the individual, and ends up not only controlling the entire polity and economy but also arts, culture, literature, etc. However, I do not recall Marx, Engels, Lenin, Stalin, and other deities of communist pantheon, or any of their theoreticians, instructing the comrades and citizens whether or not to urinate on soft ground, how to uncover private parts of the body, how to clean oneself after defecation, how to wash a tooth-stick, or what sexual position is proper. But Islam is very particular even about the most mundane and trivial of human activities; the advice of theologians is sought in such issues, as evident from Hadees and fatwas. As Shourie wrote in *The World of Fatwas*: "That a community which has been weaned on the dogma that even on such matters it needs the guidance of a Prophet has had all capacity for thinking for itself drained out of it. That a community drained in this way is ripe for picking by the *Ulema*." And it is not surprising that this community provides a never-ending source of terrorists.

Girilal Jain once wrote that the Muslim community had erected a Chinese Wall around itself. But this wall proved to be as effective, or ineffective, as was the Great Wall of China: invasions continued. Today, Islam is exposed to influences of the West; the modern among the community are painfully aware of its social backwardness, political infantilism, technological inferiority, military weaknesses, and cultural tawdriness. This has created a

strange dialectic between Islam and the West. As V.S. Naipaul wrote in *Among the Believers*:

> The West, or the universal civilization it leads, is emotionally rejected [by Muslims]. It undermines; it threatens. But at the same time it is needed, for its machines, goods, medicines, warplanes, the remittances from the emigrants, the hospitals that might have a cure for calcium deficiency, the universities that will provide master's degrees in mass media. All the rejection of the West is contained within the assumption that there will always exist out there a living, creative civilization, oddly neutral, open to all to appeal to. Rejection, therefore, is not absolute rejection. It is also, for the community as a whole, a way of ceasing to strive intellectually. It is to be parasitic; parasitism is one of the unacknowledged fruits of fundamentalism.

The same is also true for groups like the Rashtriya Swamsevak Sangh (RSS). Partly devoted to Gandhian sentimentalism, partly to "cultural nationalism", the RSS is as confused as Islam is in its response to the West. The RSS also wants to partly reject the West. However, the RSS' influence on Hindu society is marginal, though Leftist mythology has it that RSS functionaries have infiltrated everywhere. Nor does the RSS have much of a future, as Hindu society has assumed a trajectory that is beyond the ken of RSS comprehension; sooner or later, the RSS will lose whatever power or relevance it enjoys today.

But the same cannot be said about Islam. It has proved to be a laggard, not only vis-à-vis the West but also in comparison with a developing country like India. India can boast of democracy, modern institutions, a free press, a vibrant middle class, and technological prowess. The big question is: are the millions of Muslims doomed to the straitjacket of a religion that has proved to be inflexible for fourteen centuries? Many conservatives are likely to answer in the affirmative. However, my answer is "no". In this regard, I would rely on Natan Sharansky.

Sharansky's views on Islam should be preceded with a little introduction the man. Natan (Anatoly) Sharansky was born in the

Ukraine, and graduated with a degree in mathematics from the Physical Technical Institute in Moscow. His early association with the human rights movement was as an English interpreter for Andrei Sakharov, before emerging in his own right as a foremost dissident and spokesman for the Soviet Jewry movement.

In 1973, Sharansky applied for an exit visa to Israel, but was refused because of "security" reasons. He remained prominently involved in Jewish refusenik activities until his arrest in 1977. Convicted in 1978 of treason and spying on behalf of the United States, Sharansky was sentenced to thirteen years imprisonment. He spent sixteen months in Moscow's Lefortovo prison, frequently in solitary confinement and in a special "torture cell", before being transferred to a notorious prison camp in the Siberian Gulag.

During the years of his imprisonment, Sharansky became a symbol for human rights in general and Soviet Jewry in particular. A campaign for his release was waged tirelessly by his wife, Avital, who emigrated to Israel immediately after their wedding with the hope that her husband would follow shortly. Intense diplomatic efforts and public outcry for his release were unsuccessful until 1986, when Sharansky was released as part of an East-West prisoner exchange. Freed on the border of a still-divided Germany, he was met by the Israeli ambassador who presented him immediately with his new Israeli passport under the Hebrew name of Natan Sharansky. He arrived in Israel on February 11, 1986, and was greeted by leading government officials, including then Prime Minister Shimon Peres, was given a hero's welcome. He later became a cabinet minister in Israel.

In an interview, Sharansky said, "We can gain some optimism from history." He cites the example of Japan. "Truman's advisors were very skeptical about the prospects for democracy in Japan, as were most of the 'experts' of the time. And there were good reasons to be skeptical. This was a country with virtually no exposure to the West for centuries. Japan's rigidly hierarchical society, and unique culture was seen as antithetical to democratic life. In fact, when the concept of rights was translated into Japan it took a

compound word consisting of four characters to express it. But democracy in Japan has been a great success story. Japan is not a Western democracy. The Japanese have kept their traditions, culture and heritage, but they have joined the community of free nations."

In Sharansky's scheme of things, there are two kinds of societies, free societies and fear societies. "Free societies are societies in which the right of dissent is protected. In contrast, fear societies are societies in which dissent is banned. One can determine whether a society is free by applying what we call the 'town-square test'. Can someone within that society walk into the town square and say what they want without fear of being punished for his or her views? If so, then that society is a free society. If not, it is a fear society."

Further, "Fear societies are inevitably composed of three separate groups: true believers, dissidents, and double-thinkers. True believers are those who believe in the ideology of the regime. Dissidents are those who disagree with that ideology and are prepared to say so openly. Double-thinkers are those who disagree with the ideology but who are scared to openly confront the regime.

"With time, the number of double-thinkers in a fear society inevitably grows so that they represent the overwhelming majority of the population. To an outside observer, the fear society will look like a sea of true believers who demonstrate loyalty to the regime, but the reality is very different. Behind the veneer of support is an army of double-thinkers."

He sees similarity between the Japan of 1940s and the Muslim world of twenty-first century. "One only has to read the memoirs of those dissidents who have left places like Iran and Saudi Arabia to understand that these societies are steeped in doublethink. I have no doubt that, given a real choice, the vast majority of Muslims and Arabs, like everyone else, will choose a free society over a fear society. Believe me, the drug of freedom is universally potent. Once the life of double-think and self-censorship is shed, once the brainwashing stops, once freedom is tasted, no people will ever choose to live in fear again."

Unfortunately, there are many opponents of the "drug of freedom" everywhere in the world. It would be foolish to assume that in the world of Islam the mullahs are the only, or even the strongest, force against liberation; the biggest enemies are liberals and intellectuals, whose sophistry and shenanigans check the spread of Sharansky's drug.

As we mentioned earlier, the adherents of other religions have made fundamental changes in their faiths. They have analyzed and criticized the cardinal principles of their own faiths. Muslims can also follow suit. But the misguided "liberalism" and pernicious political correctness of liberals discourage the Muslims to do any self-appraisal. It is primarily because of the self-imposed blindness of liberals and intellectuals that such a closed, inequitable community is often presented as an egalitarian society.

Indian intellectuals are vociferous, often rabid, while discussing the evils of Hindu society—untouchability and satee (even though they are dying practices), dowry, female feticide, etc. But when it comes to the shortcomings of Islam, they walk on eggshells. They become extremely cautious, lest they be denigrated as knickerwallahs. They want to appear "fair" to Muslims. They end up helping jihad. Not surprisingly, the difference between their views and those of Islamic fundamentalists becomes slim. This is evident from not only their criticism of America and its war on terror but also India's reaction to Muslim violence, the madarssas, and related issues. Regrettably, the champions of liberty become apologists of Islamic fundamentalism.

10 Doublespeak of Liberal Muslims

We are often reminded that the Muslim community is in the clutches of mullahs, and this is the reason for its fanaticism and violent behavior in the community. The diabolical mullahs do not allow Muslims to go for good education and modernize themselves; Muslims remain trapped in the gridlock of ignorance, superstition, and obscurantism. Concomitantly, the voice of "liberal Muslims" is drowned in the clergy-inspired climate of opinion; liberal Muslims face Islamist McCarthyism.

In the Islamic world, we are told, an epic war is going on between good liberals and bad mullahs: the forces of secularism, humanism, compassion, and pluralism are pitted against those of theocracy, fundamentalism, terrorism, and obscurantism. One of the warriors on the side of the good, till recently, was Rafiq Zakaria, an author and columnist—the liberal Muslim *par excellence*. Another righteous warrior is Mushirul Hasan, an academic who in the early 1990s had trouble with fundamentalist youth in the Jamia Milia University in Delhi for his pro-Rushdie comment. The two scholars are among a small warrior class who are engaged in a mortal combat with the abominable mullahs.

Or so we are told.

Let's examine the well-known "liberal Muslim", Zakaria. In an article in *Mid Day*, October 16, 2002, he wrote:

> Christians right from the time of the rise of Islam have indulged in the worst forms of character assassination of the Prophet. St

> John of Damascus, soon after the death of the Prophet, mounted a campaign of denunciation by calling Muhammad an "impostor". The others who followed him used the worst epithets; they could not tolerate the success of Islam, which spread at their cost everywhere.
>
> When the new religion reached almost the heart of Europe, most Christians lost their balance . . .
>
> Frustrated Christian monks hurled the vilest abuses on Muhammad and the *Koran*. The situation became even worse after the Crusades. The Church led the campaign of hate, with Christian writers and poets following suit. The anti-Islamic literature of medieval times is a painful and pathetic reflection on Christian bigotry.

Christians "could not tolerate the success of Islam, which spread at their cost everywhere". With such liberals, does Islam need any bigots? Incidentally, Islam spread not only at the cost Christianity but all great religions like Hinduism or Buddhism; and nowhere was the spread because of, as Zakaria claims, Mohammad's "immense contribution" to human redemption. However, let's restrict ourselves here to the success of Islam against Christianity. At the time of Islam's origination in Arabia in the seventh century, the entire north Africa, Egypt, Palestine, Lebanon, Syria, and Asia Minor (now Turkey) were Christian. In his *Islam Unveiled*, Robert Spencer says: "It is undeniable that Muslims won these lands by conquest and, in obedience to the words of the Qur'an and the Prophet, put to sword the infidels therein who refused to submit to the new Islamic regime. Those who escaped their fate lived in humiliating second-class status. Conversion to Islam became the only way to have a decent life. Not surprisingly, the Christian populations of those areas steadily diminished."

One of the greatest authorities on Islam in contemporary times, Bernard Lewis, corroborates Spencer's conclusion. According to Lewis, "When the Crusaders arrived in Jerusalem, barely hundred years had passed since that city, along with the rest of the Levant and North Africa, had been wrested by the armies of Islam from

their Christian rulers, and their Christian populations forcibly incorporated in a new Muslim empire. The Crusade was a delayed response to the jihad, the holy war for Islam, and its purpose was to recover by war what had been lost by war—to free the holy places of Christendom and open them once again, without impediment, to Christian pilgrimage."

Even *Encyclopedia Britannica*, which downplays Islam's ferocity in dealing with infidels, could not ignore Prophet Mohammad's misdeeds: "After the siege of Medina, Muhammad attacked the Jewish clan of Qurazah, which had probably been intriguing against him. When they surrendered, the men were all executed and the women and children sold as slaves." Further, it says: "Some of the evidence against him such as his connivance at assassinations and his approval of the execution of the men of Jewish clan, are historical matters that *cannot be denied*" (emphasis added). So much for Mohammad's "immense contribution" to human uplift.

Rafiq Zakaria, a "liberal Muslim", obviously wants to ignore or bury these facts—that is, if he considers them as "facts" in the first place. Like many neo-Nazis who refuse to accept the reality of Holocaust, he seems to be negating rather than downplaying these facts. To cover one lie, they say, you have to speak a hundred more. One such Zakaria's novel new interpretation of Hindu-Muslim conflict:

> In short, animosity of all classes of Christians against Muhammad is endemic; they have never accepted him as a true prophet or his immense contribution to human upliftment (*sic*). The epithets may have been modified in recent times but these erupt in one form or the other every now and again. In injecting the hatred against Muhammad among the Hindus, the British played the decisive role. Until their advent in India there existed in none of the Indian languages any diatribe against Muhammad; it is the British governors and Christian missionaries who did all the dirty work to prejudice Hindus against the Prophet.

Notice how terms "Christians" and "British" are used interchangeably in Zakaria's discourse. This is another conspiracy theory: Leftist and Muslim intellectuals cannot live without conspiracy theories. We are told by the Left historians that the British were responsible for every possible problem India currently suffers from—from poverty to bureaucracy. Now comes one more charge, and not just against the British imperialists but also against "Christian missionaries" (however, if such an allegation is made by Praveen Togadia, then that is blatant communalism!).

This is a typical response of not only Muslim intellectuals but also other insular and inward-looking groups like the Sangh Parivar: blame everything on somebody else, preferably the West. Why do Muslims use terrorist means? The Rafiq Zakarias reply promptly: because they are poor, and terrorism is the poor man's way of making his presence felt. But there is little correlation between poverty and terrorism; terrorist organizations like Babbar Khalsa and Jaish-e-Mohammad exist not in the poorest regions of the country such as Kalahandi and Bolangir. Further, the 18-odd terrorists who carried out September 11 attacks were certainly not poor. Neither is Osama bin Laden. But such facts are ignored.

Unsurprisingly, in this make-believe world, deception and self-deception come with great alacrity. In another article, in *Hindustan Times* (October 21, 2001), Zakaria wrote: "the hold on the Muslims of the liberals and progressives is on the increase; the youth is quietly responding to them. Progressive Islam is on the march. In the larger interest of our nation, the media should not ignore it."

Could anything be farther from the truth? Anybody who has eyes and ears, and an iota of commonsense, can comprehend that the mullah is increasingly becoming stronger and more dangerous, as he has the capability to attract the youth. The developments following the Islamic Revolution in Iran in 1979 have made the ulema extremely strong and influential. From Pakistan to Indonesia, from former Soviet Central Asian republics to the Muslim community in the US, the mullah's hold has remained undiminished.

In Mushirul Hasan, eloquence and poetry embellish deception and self-deception. He wrote an article, "A Return to Iqbal's New Temple," in *The Indian Express* (October 2, 2002):

> Nurturing the vision of a new temple that would "give all worshippers the wine of love to drink," he [Iqbal] concludes his powerful plea with the following lines:
> There is power, there is peace in the songs of the devotees—
> The salvation of all dwellers on the earth is love.

Hasan also mentioned Hasrat Mohani and a medieval Sufi poet. He wrote:

> Love, religious tolerance and mutual respect for religious sites are the keywords, for they convey the long-standing trajectory of our society. In this respect, I am reminded of Hasrat Mohani (1878-1951), the Urdu poet, journalist and politician . . . .
> The other outstanding figure is Shah Abdur Razzaq (1637-1724). Throughout his life, he encouraged by his words and actions a liberal and conciliatory approach to local Hindu religious rites and social practices. His principal concern was to maintain and enhance amicable relations between the diverse communities, even though some of his preferences violated the sharia. Two of his major disciples and his son had a special fondness for the bhakti-baz song and dance sequence depicting the life of Narasimha Avatar and Krishna. Indeed, it was in the full knowledge of their spiritual preceptor that they once watched bhaktiyas performing the life of Krishna, at the home of Chait Ram and Paras Ram, the bairagis.

All this is fine; in fact, there are many more instances in which Muslim poets and Sufi saints made genuine efforts to bridge the gulf between the Hindu and Muslim communities; and these efforts were reciprocated by bhakti saints and poets. But is "religious tolerance" a keyword for Muslims, as Hasan claims? And the answer is an emphatic no—in India, as elsewhere.

But Hasan persists. In another article, "Looking Ahead with Fear," (*The Indian Express*, September 18, 2002), he wrote about the victims of September 11:

> We mourn their death and condemn the perpetrators of the cold-blooded murder.
>
> If we are to escape such unimaginable catastrophes, it was hoped that the US would find a way of dealing with the reasons that give birth to terrorist outfits and that it would garner Muslim support in its monumental struggle against terrorism. This has not happened. Indeed, belligerence rather than sober reflection has been the dominant refrain of US foreign policy. Wielding the big stick, the administration flouts its own rules and norms in Kashmir, Afghanistan, Iraq and Palestine. Time and time again, its policies tend to inflame rather than soothe religious passions.

Hasan heaps all blame for September 11 on the US—for its failure to find "the reasons that give birth to terrorist outfits"; US "policies tend to inflame rather than soothe religious passions". In short, the victim is the villain. It's an old tactic: justify terrorism by taking recourse to "the reasons that give birth" to terrorism, by harping on the "root cause", by pointing out social and economic factors. Why did Mumbai blasts happen in 1993? Because of the demolition of Babri Masjid on December 6, 1992. Why the blast bombs in Mumbai in 2003? Because of the Gujarat riots in 2002. Muslims, and Islam, are never responsible for terrorism; everybody else is.

The constant refrain of the likes of Hasan is that all Muslims are not terrorists. This is of course true, but what they do not explain is why most terrorists are Muslims. As Victor Davis Hanson wrote in *National Review* on December 5, 2003 (A Real War): "even apart from all the killing in Israel and Iraq, *all* of the deadly terrorism since 9/11—the synagogue in Tunisia, French naval personnel in Pakistan, Americans in Karachi, Yemeni attacks on a French ship, the Bali bombing, the Kenyan attack on Israelis, the several deadly attacks on Russians in both Moscow and Chechnya, the assault on housing compounds in Saudi Arabia, the sui-

cide car bombing in Morocco, the Marriott bombing in Indonesia, the mass murdering in Bombay, and the Turkish killing—has been perpetrated exclusively by Muslim fascists and directed at Westerners, Christians, Hindus, and Jews." Isn't this a clash of civilizations? A clash between Islam and the rest?

Mushirul Hasan's answer is no. According to him:

> Islamist outfits ran for cover in the aftermath of September 11. They stood discredited among Muslims and their version of Islam was powerfully repudiated by scores of clerics and theologians. Egypt, Saudi Arabia, Turkey, Afghanistan, Pakistan—to mention just a few countries—moved against them in a determined bid to destroy their support base.
>
> In reality, the threat from Islamic militants is a figment of somebody's wild imagination in the White House.

One wonders whether this is deception or self-deception. Islamist outfits "discredited"!? These are the outfits that governments all over the world dread. Such organizations are especially the bane of the Muslim world; from Indonesia to the Middle East to Europe, the authorities in Muslim countries are finding it difficult to tackle such outfits, primarily because they are popular among the Muslims; they are anything but discredited.

And is Hasan in his right senses when he says that "the threat from Islamic militants is a figment of somebody's wild imagination in the White House"? Now, being anti-American is one thing, but accusing it of everything under the sun is clearly a case of hate psychosis.

Contradicting himself, Hasan makes a few amends:

> Likewise, there is no denying the force and appeal of Islamic fundamentalism, of which Talibanisation is a crude manifestation. Yet other variants of the same ideology have expressed themselves with equal force and vigor: in Israel, Sri Lanka, Bosnia-Herzegovina, Kosovo, Chechnya, and the riot-torn cities of Gujarat. The difference, one that comes in handy for Islam-baiters, is that they are categorized differently. Thus, the murder

> of scores of Palestinian women and children is not an act of terrorism; the death of a few Israelis is.
>
> What has the US administration done since 9/11 to soothe tempers? It endorses Israel's military occupation of Palestine, fabricates a case against Iraq to capture its rich oilfields, and adopts an adversarial posture towards Iran. This being the case, I suspect that the US president's mindset will encourage rather than deter the Islamists from striking at their adversaries in the West. The invasion of Iraq, as and when it happens, will be the last straw. Besides breeding fierce resentment among Muslims, who wish to co-exist peacefully with the West, it will be construed as a war against Islam. It will bring the jehadis out in the open.

Finally, Hasan does accept that abominations like Islamic fundamentalism and Taliban do exist, this comes with a peculiar subterfuge, the subterfuge that can be called "linkism"—that is, all depredations of Islam are linked to something or the other. In any case, why did Muslims carry out the September 11 attacks? Because of the wrong policies of the US in the Middle East: the onus is again on somebody else, this time the victim. Why is there hardly any democracy in any Muslim country? Because the US promotes dictatorships in Muslim countries. Why and how did the Taliban, Mullah Omar, and Osama come to power in Afghanistan? Because the US quit as soon as its objective of ousting the Soviets was achieved (They would also have accused the US, this time of neo-imperialism, had it decided to stay on in Afghanistan after the withdrawal of the Soviet troops!). Why do Muslims become terrorists? Because Others goad them to do so. And the Others are everywhere—Jews in Israel, Hindus in India, racists in the UK, imperialists in the US. Terrorists are also everywhere—in Israel there are the Zionists, in Sri Lanka the Tigers, in Bosnia and Kosovo Christians, in Chechnya (apparently) the Russians, and in Gujarat there is Narendra Modi. The fact, however, is that there is an enormous difference of scale and scope between Islamic terrorists and the so-called terrorists mentioned by Hasan. Firstly, Islamic terror is global. Secondly, it is incorrigible. For the Muslims

can check Islamic terror effectively only if they are willing to edit the *Koran*. That would require not just exegesis but a fundamental revision of their faith because, according to Islam, the *Koran* is the word of Allah. And, in any case, there are no signs of such revision: Muslims, fundamentalist as well as liberal, continue to justify their faith by calling it peaceful; and non-Muslim liberals all over the world gullibly accept such lies as the truths of multiculturalism.

Hasan continues his affair with falsehoods and lies. In another article in, "The Year of Strife," *The Indian Express* (September 4, 2002), he wrote:

> September 11 is too close for comfort. On that fateful day, a group of misguided persons attacked the World Trade Center and the Pentagon. Whatever their motives or source of inspiration, they should never have done that. All of us have strong feelings about one or the other issue, but there is no justification for spreading our creed by force of arms. The death of scores of innocent civilians trapped in a tower or an office inevitably leads to widespread fear, despair and anger.
>
> The perpetrators of the attack—give them any name you like—have accomplished nothing. Their icon, Osama bin Laden, is either dead or probably tasting dust in a bottomless pit. The authoritarian and feudal regimes he targeted are intact, and probably better equipped to suppress dissent. In fact, the worldwide coalition against terrorism has rescued them from the brink of a precipice. Democratic movements, that are at any rate weak in the Arab world, have been a major casualty after September 11. This is Al-Qaeda's doing. A military dictator who introduces a constitutional amendment periodically to eliminate potential rivals rules Pakistan. Instead of being upbraided by the custodians of democracy, he receives testimonials of good conduct from Washington.

Hasan got it all wrong. To begin with, the September 11 attacks did not kill just "scores of innocent civilians trapped"; the death count was more than 3,000; this is another instance how the so-

called liberal Muslims downplay the depredations of jihadists. Further, democratic movements were *not* "a major casualty after September 11" in the Arab or Muslim world; in the first place, they did not exist in the sense the West and India are familiar with: that is, a political system in which the government is responsible to the people, where an open society exists, where human rights and civil liberties are respected, where gender equality is a reality, where minorities are protected. On September 10, 2001, out of more than four dozen Muslim states only Turkey, Bangladesh, and Indonesia, were democracies. Even these three countries could not be called proper democracies. In Turkey, the army was the backbone of democracy and secularism, keeping in check the Islamists. However, such is the nature of Islam that almost after a century of Kamal Mustafa Ataturk's influence, non-Muslim populations have consistently declined. Ditto with Bangladesh, which has witnessed the successful ethnic cleansing of Hindus and where millions of non-Muslims have ceased to exist, thanks to large-scale murder, conversions, or forced evictions. Indonesia, too, has been a troubled democracy, with Islamic fundamentalism raising its ugly head.

Hasan refuses to accept such facts and continues to live in his own world. According to him:

> For one, Osama's action was immediately seen as a threat to the hopes of all who share the aspirations which have inspired human progress. He, therefore, became the object of universal hate. Muslim countries rallied around the coalition against the Al-Qaeda, for its Islamist rhetoric threatened them as much as the western establishments. Muslim public opinion, such as it exists, also realized the futility of their adventure. Today, the cry goes out—from North Africa to the Indonesian archipelago—that Osama has brought nothing but pain and discomfort to the Muslims. Islam is demonized and equated, falsely of course, with terrorism, while the conduct of its believers is closely scrutinized. Hence, the newspaper coverage of numerous cases of individual harassment and intimidation. Arguably, Osama had hoped to diminish future occasions of strife in Muslim countries. If so, he

was tragically mistaken. The war in Chechnya goes on, and the US State Department, having concluded an entente cordiale with President Putin, turns a blind eye to Russia's military occupation. The same people, who suffered so much during the Holocaust, prolong the Palestinian agony. Here is a classic example of justice being inordinately delayed as well as woefully denied.

Osama the object of *universal* hate? Do Muslims hate him? All empirical evidence suggests that he is the icon of most Muslims, and seen as a leading light of Islam. Even before September 11 he had become a hero in Pakistan. There were a number of reports that in the north-western frontiers of Pakistan—that is, the area neighboring Afghanistan where he was residing at that time—Osama had become a common name of the new-born sons. Not only that, many shops, bakeries, etc, were named after Osama. According to a survey carried out in Pakistan by *The Economist* in the aftermath of September 11, about 83 per cent of the people supported the attacks on WTC and the Pentagon. All of us saw Muslims celebrating in the streets at the news of these attacks. In the protest marches against the US attack on Afghanistan, the posters of Osama were visible. Osama may have brought "pain and discomfort to the Muslims", but he remains a hero for the majority. There is no contradiction in these two facts. The analogy of Hitler's Germany is a suitable one: the Germans suffered because of him, but there is no evidence that there was any popular movement to oust him.

But Hasan is not willing to see facts; he blames everybody but Muslims for all that is wrong in the world. Israel deserves the harshest treatment:

> The Palestinians, who are no jehadis, have been wronged by history and contemporary politics. They demand nothing but the right to nationhood. They ask for nothing but the territories they lost to Israel in the 1967 war. Somebody must have the patience to listen to their woes. Somebody must persuade Israel to learn to live with the Palestinians and substitute argument for brute force. Has 9-11 altered the US policy perceptions in West Asia? It

> would appear that the "terror" factor has prompted the administration to delegitimise Palestinian groups, notably Al-Hamas, by stigmatizing them as "terrorist". It has also stiffened its resolve to maintain the status quo in West Asia. No wonder, the Republican administration has come out strongly in support of Ariel Sharon, a megalomanic Zionist, and against Yasser Arafat, a freedom fighter with impeccable credentials. In short, the US will not offer any tangible concessions to the Palestinians unless it can extract its pound of flesh from the wealthy and strategically well-placed Arab nations.

Notice that, in Hasan's scheme of things, the US administration has been "stigmatizing" Al-Hamas as a terrorist organization (as if the leaders and activists of Al-Hamas were the disciples of Mahatma Gandhi!). Also notice that Ariel Sharon is "a megalomaniac Zionist", while Yasser Arafat is a "freedom fighter with impeccable credentials". Could anything be farther from the truth? A world-famous terrorist is glorified as a freedom fighter! And a democratically elected prime minister is demonized! All this by an academic who is lionized in India as a "liberal Muslim".

If there is one issue that evokes a similar reaction from Hasan, it is Gujarat. In another article, Recovering the Lost Ground, in *The Indian Express* (May 1, 2002), he wrote:

> Today, India stands partitioned—not territorially but in terms of the polarization that has taken place across the board. The swing of the electoral fortunes may temporarily reverse this process, but that may not bring about the meeting of minds and the mending of hearts. After Gujarat, the second partition has occurred, exposing the weakness of secular goals and policies. Recovering the secular ground is, admittedly, a compelling necessity, but the turf, vandalized by the Sangh Parivar, is not, at present, easy to negotiate . . .
>
> Rooted in the ideas and movements of late-19th century reformism and essentially designed to demonize the Muslim and Islam, Hindu nationalism released its own energy to capture the minds of its potential adherents in urban areas. Seemingly dor-

> mant owing to the Congress' hegemonic presence, it surfaced in the 1940s to counter the Pakistan idea, an idea that the RSS, the Hindu Mahasabha and the Arya Samaj had itself cultivated by imaging the Muslims as the Other. With its cultural and religious baggage gifted by the Orientalist scholars, Hindu nationalism gained a fresh lease of life in the late 1880s, directing its anger, once again, against the minorities. The pogrom organized in Gujarat has, from the standpoint of its votaries, advanced the project pioneered by no other than the Gujarati-born Dayanand Saraswati. His book, *Satyarth Prakash*, is a classic exposition of the pungently divisive ideas that are now being articulated in Hindutva circles.
>
> . . . Islam is not just a religion but a tremendous civilizational force; it will remain so despite the massacre of Palestinians, the plight of the Iraqis, and the trauma of Gujarati Muslims. Secularism, though assailed by the votaries of Hindutva, is not yet a defeated idea in civil society. It still commands, moreover, the allegiance of the non-BJP political classes. Let me also reiterate that a secular polity is the sole guarantor of our survival as a community and the nation.

So, you see, it is the Hindus who have been behind every evil. They are responsible for the vivisection of the country, not once but twice—first, in 1947 and then again in 2002. They "demonize the Muslim and Islam"; they direct their anger against the minorities; they organize pogroms in Gujarat and elsewhere. Taking recourse to the victim-is-the-villain doctrine, fashionable among Leftist and liberal circles, Hasan heaps all blame on Hindu organizations—the RSS, the Hindu Mahasabha, the Arya Samaj.

Forget the truths of history; in any case, history has always been a target of Leftist and Muslim scholars, relentlessly distorted and muddled by these purveyors of myths. But such interpretation, that Hindu nationalism was the cause of Partition, is a weird innovation even by the acceptable standards of mendacious scholarship—acceptable, of course, in the ivory towers of political correctness and the rarefied environs of academics and academia. So, forget Rahmat Ali who coined the term "Pakistan"; forget Iqbal,

who added poetic gloss to the idea; forget Sir Syed Ahmad Khan, his anti-Hindu diatribe, and his avowal of Muslim separatism; forget Jinnah and forget Liaqat Ali Khan; also forget Suhrawardy, the butcher of Calcutta; forget the venomous mullah whose vituperation caused so many riots; forget Congress pusillanimity and stupidity in tackling Muslim separatism; forget Jawaharlal Nehru's bungling and indecent haste to acquire power. Remember only Hindu nationalism—the bane of India. This is the message of Mushirul Hasan, the great liberal Muslim of contemporary India, supposedly an intellectual giant, a darling of the media.

Peddling lies and distorting the truth is the hallmark of Hasan, Rafiq Zakaria, and many other so-called liberal Muslims. They receive considerable support from the media, which is controlled by great liberals and intellectuals, mostly from the Left. Not surprisingly, Hasan accepts this support with gratitude: "The silver lining in this otherwise dismal picture is the role of the media and the activism of the secular forces, led by Left-wing parties and groups."

The romance between the media and the peddlers of lies continues unabated.

11 P. Chidambaram
Borrowing from the Left

Finance Minister P. Chidambaram is seen as one of the champions of liberalization, of market economy. As Finance Minister in the United Front government (1996-98), he is said to have continued the process of economic reforms, which was heralded by Manmohan Singh. The Budget he presented in 1998 was hailed by industry as a "dream budget". In short, Chidambaram, an ace lawyer, is one man who should view the agenda of the Left with suspicion.

But he doesn't. In fact, he picks up certain items of the Leftist agenda, and then unquestioningly adopts them. For instance, he supports the essentially illiberal concept of empowerment in all its forms including affirmative action. Supporting reservation for women in legislative bodies, he wrote in *The Indian Express* ("Women's Bill: No Reservation, Just Bias," May 11, 2003):

> There are serious issues of gender justice that have not yet been tackled in this country. First and foremost, is the declining ratio of females to males. In all the States of the country—except Kerala—there are fewer women than men, and the ratio has worsened in the decades since Independence.
>
> If we look at the infant mortality rate (IMR), we find that, in some districts of India, the IMR of female children is six times that of male children. In rural areas there are more centers for

> scanning than dental clinics. All these are clear pointers to the widespread prevalence of female infanticide.
>
> As the girl child grows up, she faces insurmountable hurdles compared to boys. She spends fewer years in school. Most girl children have less access to higher education compared to boys. She has also less access to food or medical care. At every step and every turn in life, she faces handicaps unique to her gender.

He cannot be faulted in recognizing the problem; it is the remedy he suggests that is worse than the malady. Chidambaram's remedy, or rather panacea, is affirmative action.

The Women's Reservation Bill is a bid to empower women, to open a fast and exclusive track so that some women can enter Parliament and take their rightful place in the governance of the country.

Interestingly, Chidambaram is aware of the hollowness of the empowerment argument. He writes:

> I have no illusions that governance will become better or more just and humane. As many women public servants are booked for corruption as men. And the record of our women Chief Ministers—Rabri Devi, Jayalalithaa and Mayawati—is nothing to be proud about. Their craving for power and money seems, at least for the present, unmatched by their male counterparts!

However, he continues chant the mantra of reservations for women.

But the point is that men have no business to judge women. As long as political parties are dominated by men, they will find a hundred excuses to keep out women.

If Chidambaram has no illusions about the "the craving for power and money" of women politicians, why does he support their cause? Even though he accepts the absence of any arguments in *favor* of women empowerment, he writes:

> There are, in fact, no arguments *against* the Women's Reservation Bill. The only unarticulated argument is the fear of the male

> politician that he would have to yield space to women. Since he cannot voice that argument, he gives full play to his lung power. It is a pity that the Prime Minister and the Speaker meekly submitted to a prejudiced minority. [emphasis added]

This is nothing but political correctness, without any adulteration of reason and commonsense. Which is not inappropriate after all, since the name of the column is "Politically Correct".

Chidambaram blindly accepts a few Leftist doctrines. The most important one is that of social engineering: the society is a machine that can be engineered as per the need of the hour. This is incorrect, for society is an organism rather than a machine. The consequences of social engineering are for all to see: the Nazis wanted to engineer a society, ruled by the Master Race, and this resulted in the slaughter of millions of Jews, Poles, gypsies, and other peoples; the communist wanted to set up classless societies in various parts of the world, and this caused the deaths of millions of people.

Affirmative action is the child of social engineering. Reservations, based on birth-based criterion (of gender, caste, or community), have proved to be failure in our country, as also elsewhere. There is little evidence to prove that more than half a century of affirmative action in favor of scheduled castes and tribes has caused any improvement in their lot. This is not to suggest that there has been no improvement; but this has been because of modernization and development.

Fifty years of affirmative action has only produced leaders like Ram Vilas Paswan and Meira Kumar—leaders who are the antithesis of development and progress, leaders who have a vested interest in keeping their less fortunate brethren poor and uneducated, leaders who are unable to think beyond the politics of marginalization, the politics of reservations, leaders whose contribution to the nation is zero, if not negative.

These days the champions of reservations peg their arguments on two assumptions. First, uplift of any group or community is possible only with help from the State. Second, a "deprived" class

can be redeemed only if its members occupy high offices. Both assumptions are of doubtful validity.

To begin with, the state has always been an impediment rather than a facilitator of development. The West is successful because it has managed, more or less, to keep the state under leash; it has learnt its lessons at a great cost, Nazi Germany and communist Russia being the biggest instances of big state. Broadly speaking, the entire world is witnessing the rollback of state from economy, be it democratic societies like India and Sri Lanka or communist China.

The second assumption is most insular in nature, for it divides mankind into myriad watertight communities, all at war with on another; uplift is possible only by intra-community action; inter-community dialogue or cooperation is ruled out. Upper caste people help each other; so do the backward classes, dalits, Muslims, etc. The assumption is wrong. For one, it does not explain the motivation of people who think of mankind as a whole, and not in parochial terms. Raja Ram Mohan Roy, Swami Dayanand, Ishwarchand Vidyasagar, Swami Vivekanand, Mahatma Gandhi—each of them singly did more for the uplift of depressed classes than all the contemporary "messiahs" of the poor and dalits put together. This despite the fact that all of them were from upper castes, and many came from the hated Brahmin community.

An educated person like Chidambaram is surely not unaware of this, but he continues to ignore these facts; he chooses, instead, to mouth Leftist shibboleths. Since anti-Americanism is the leitmotif of Leftist rhetoric, he merrily joins in the chorus bashing the United States. In an article, "Vietnam a Blot, Iraq a Scar" (*The Indian Express*, April 13, 2003), he wrote:

> The United States was never a colonizer. Its record in the immediate post-Second World War period was a proud one that exemplified the core values of America. Over the years, that record has been tarnished. Vietnam was a huge blot, now Iraq will remain an indelible scar. The people of countries that admired the US or even envied the US will, in the future, fear the US and the increasing arrogance of the world's sole superpower.

Chidambaram is mistaken: howsoever proud America's role may have been in any period, few in the world admire the US. At any rate, the Leftists, whose wisdom he has internalized, have never admired the US. The Leftists will continue to revile the US—and liberals like Chidambaram would follow suit—because they hate "the core values of America". It was these core values that motivated America to go to Vietnam in the first place. Vietnam was not a blot, for the US did not go there to colonize; the idea was to contain communism, the biggest evil mankind has ever witnessed. The core values and the cherished ideals of individual liberty, limited government, free market, and open society were threatened by communism.

It was not the presence of American forces but their *withdrawal* from Vietnam that created problems. It emboldened Leftist and other anti-American elements all over the world. The most tragic consequence was the rise of the barbarous Pol Pot regime in Cambodia that killed more than three million people, eliminating one out of seven people in the poor country.

The Vietnam War became a scandal because the liberals in America blindly accepted the loony theories of the likes of Chomsky and created a furor; participation in anti-war demonstrations became chic; and pacifism became fashionable. The Left, with ample support from the liberal establishment, went in an overdrive to undermine the core values of America in the 1960s and 1970s. It was only when Ronald Reagan came to power in 1980 that the tide turned. With great support from Margaret Thatcher of the UK, Reagan's US was able to call the communist bluff, and this led to the collapse of the Soviet Union and the end of communism as a global threat. This also acted as a catalyst for India to break free of the shackles of socialist economy to a large extent and the adoption of market economy in 1991.

Former Disinvestment Minister Arun Shourie once said that there is a "consensus in practice" over the issue of privatization. All political parties favor the sale of public sector undertakings (PSUs), from the Congress to the communists of West Bengal. But they resist privatization when they are in Opposition. So, the

Congressmen and communists resisted the sale of Central PSUs by the NDA government, but they had no compunctions in privatizing the PSUs in the states where they ruled. Punjab, Madhya Pradesh, Karnataka, Chhattisgarh, and West Bengal are some of the states which have been privatizing state PSUs. But they are not the only hypocrites. The ruling BJP is no better. It promoted privatization at the Centre when it was in power (1998-2004), but when the Delhi state government privatized Delhi Vidyut Board, BJP leader Madan Lal Khurana raised a stink.

But it is not just privatization where hypocrisy prevails; the entire liberalization process is marred by it. The good thing about liberalization is that it has been promoted by whichever party has held power at the Centre since 1991, and this covers a wide range of the ideological spectrum—from the supposedly Rightwing Vajpayee government to the Centrist Congress to the Left-of-Centre United Front. Fortunately, liberalization has been the policy of government since 1991, whichever party had ruled since then; but, unfortunately, on all issues socialism has been the rhetoric of the Opposition, whichever political party has been in the Opposition. The problem is that rhetoric catches the imagination of not only the political class but also of the people.

On the US' Iraq war in 2003, Chidambaram wrote,

> India's response to the 23-day war (so far) was pathetic and laughable. Countries like France and Germany, which are more closely tied to the US, particularly through NATO, did not hesitate to warn the US against starting a war without UN approval. The Pope did not flinch from condemning the US, a Christian nation, for waging a war against Iraq, an Islamic country.

In short, Chidambaramm wants India to continue US-bashing it has indulged in since Independence.

Jawaharlal Nehru, a quintessential guilt-ridden socialist politician, disliked America. Yet, his anti-Americanism never completely endeared him to the communists who, at one point, called him the "running dog of imperialism". But the more the communists hated Nehru and the more the Left lambasted him, the more

he tried to win them over. His alter ego, V.K. Krishna Menon, capitalized on Nehru's psychology. Menon, who held the important portfolios of British High Commissioner, Defence Minister, and Ambassador to the United Nations, transformed diplomacy into theatrics and the foreign office into a front organization of the erstwhile Soviet Union. The legacy of Nehru and Menon survives, even after the demise of Soviet Union more than a decade ago. That legacy has now found new adherents—Chidambaram is one of them. He writes:

> Saddam Hussein is not my hero, he deserved to fall, but not through the hand of a self-appointed global policeman. The tragedy of Iraq will haunt mankind for many years.

This is in the best traditions of Leftist obfuscation: "I condemn the September 11 attacks, but the US must think why the world hates it"; "There were some excesses in the Soviet Union and China, but . . . "; "The blowing up of the Buddha's statue in Bamiyan is deplorable, but . . . "; "The Muslim community has a lunatic fringe, but . . . ."

And, like any good liberal, Chidambaram has to cry about Gujarat at one time or the other. He does it in an article, "At Stake, India As a Civilized Society" (*The Indian Express*, September 29, 2002). He wrote:

> The nation may perhaps survive if our individual hates and prejudices remain private and under control. But if each one of us gangs up with those who share the same hates and prejudices, and together unleash violence upon others, can the nation survive? For many years, we harbored the comforting illusion that such collective expression of prejudice was a failing of the poor, the unemployed and the illiterate. Gujarat shattered that illusion. Pictures of middle-class and wealthy residents of Ahmedabad raiding shops and carrying away the loot in their cars exploded the myth that we are a civilized society.
>
> Post-Gujarat, I have witnessed how shame, remorse and contriteness have vanished from the so-called civilized sections of society. Friends have told me about their friends who justified

> the violence in Gujarat .... There were reports of doctors boycotting or refusing to serve patients belonging to a certain community. It seemed as if the hates and prejudices at the individual level had been raised to a collective level, and there was no longer any sense of shame in giving expression to those dark and despicable instincts.
>
> What has the Government done in these past four years? By word and action, it has enshrined "majoritarian" values as Indian values. It has set up Pakistan as an object of hate—and the source of all our troubles, be it a train accident or a temple attack.

Notice how beautifully general sermonizing about "our individual hates and prejudices" cruises to Gujarat; and one need not be a scholar to know that Chidambaram is trying to explode the "myth" of the "civilized society" of the Hindus. Hindu society is ruthless, insensitive, and barbaric, the ace lawyer says, adding that Hindus justify the killings of Muslims, even well-to-do Hindus rob Muslims, their doctors do not attend to Muslims. In short, Hindus have "dark and despicable instincts".

Notice also that not a word has come about Godhra, or about the million atrocities committed by the Muslims on non-Muslims all over the world.

Chidambaram does not stop his essay in abuse here; he blames the Vajpayee government for setting "up Pakistan as an object of hate—and the source of all our troubles, be it a train accident or a temple attack". But what else is Pakistan? The wide world—including the US administration, the global media, even the Pakistan press—recognizes that today Pakistan is heavily under the influence of Islamists. Yet, Chidambaram does not recognize such simple facts. The reason is that except on the issues related to economy, he is in agreement with the Left. As we noticed, his views on America, Muslims, etc, are no different from those of the Left.

Chidambaram is not alone in the half-Left-half-Right quandary. Swaminathan S Anklesaria Aiyar, another champion of market economy, is in the same boat. He, too, loses his sense of proportion when discussing Gujarat. He wrote an article, "Al-Qaida Is

Already Here," in *The Times of India* on December 7, 2003, that India ceased to be a secular democracy after—well, you guessed it right—the Gujarat riots in 2002. According to Aiyar:

> The 1983 Mumbai blasts could be explained away as the work of the Muslim underground led by Dawood Ibrahim. But the latest blasts involve Muslim doctors, engineers, computer professionals and even MBAs. No longer can we explain away bomb blasts as the work of foreigners or the underground. The problem has now spread to the Muslim mainstream, including highly educated and sophisticated Muslims.
>
> This is not the result of fundamentalist preachers misleading gullible Muslims. It is the *outcome of the crassest Hindu outrages* in Gujarat. These were the first communal riots to be captured live on TV, and so they had a far deeper impact than any previous conflagrations. The unabashed communal hate displayed by sundry Hindus on TV must have infuriated the most moderate Muslims. [emphasis added]

So, you see, it is the Hindus who are at the root of every problem! And, again, in the best traditions of liberal mendacity, not one word about Godhra, or about other outrages perpetrated by the Muslims. Not a word about the plight of Kashmiri pundits, many of whom were butchered by Islamic terrorists and the others forced to flee their native land. No concern for the ethnic clearing of Hindus from Bangladesh. And not one word about the nature of Islam, which goads Muslims to murder non-Muslims, which exhorts them to wage jehad.

Being a true descendant of Gandhari, Aiyar continues to express his indignation:

> The party that spearheaded the mass murder was re-elected with a huge majority. India has a moth-eaten, perverted form of democracy that looks as oppressive to some Muslims as the worst democracies of the Middle East. The same sort of outraged Muslims that strike at American civilian targets are now striking at Indian ones.

Indian democracy is "moth-eaten" and "perverted"—and, presumably, in the entire Muslim world democracy is thriving! Perhaps unwittingly, Aiyar has exonerated the perpetrators of September 11, for they too were merely "outraged Muslims". Why were they outraged? He doesn't explain, nor does the Left, though they explain it away by screaming something about Israel. And once the word "Israel" enters the debate, there is a spurt of weird conspiracy theories about an omnipotent and omnipresent Zionist lobby, the military-industrial complex, and neo-imperialism; the result is the demise of reason and commonsense.

What is Aiyar's message? "We must revamp our democratic and secular institutions to provide protection and redressal (*sic*) to all groups." Could Prakash Karat, general secretary of the Communist Party of India (Marxist), have disagreed with the votary of capitalism?

In fact, all those who advocate market economy are not allergic to the Leftist views on politics, arts, culture, or literature; they continue to mouth the theories and ideals, slogans and clichés of the Left, often with undiminished zeal. What these worthies do not realize is the fact that the world of the Left is a seamless web, that you can't agree with one important aspect of their ideology and reject the others. For the Left is a negation, a negation of how the human world is flourishing, how the economy is growing, how the society is blossoming, how human institutions are evolving; the Left despises all this. It is not happy with how the things *are*; it wants the human world to behave in a particular fashion; the Left does everything to conform the reality to Theory, a few million deaths is merely collateral damage.

The liberals like Chidambaram and Swaminathan Aiyar may say that they are not doctrinaire enthusiasts of free market, that they are not bothered about the abstruse formulations of the Left and the Right, that they just embrace any doctrine they feel is good for mankind. They find merit in Rightwing economics; so, they espouse market. But they also find merit in political ideas of the Left; hence their support for such ideas. We are broadminded and unprejudiced, not dogmatic, they may claim.

But the problem with such broadmindedness is that it is unduly deferential to Leftist certitudes and communist theories. The Indian liberal makes it a point to prove his distance from Hindutva, even anything related to Hinduism, lest he be targeted as communal, bigoted, and fascistic. To use a term popularized by Irving Kristol, the Indian liberal is more anti-anti-communist than anti-communist.

Now, if a liberal accepts the politics of the Left, he also has to accept, broadly, its understanding of the society. And in the Indian context, this has serious consequences: the pornography of caste passes off as sociology and political analysis; a liberal has to, wittingly or unwittingly, hate India, especially Hindu India, and end up as recommending affirmative action. I am not sure if Chidambaram hates Hindu India as much as the Left does, but the remedy he has in mind, more reservations, is not only poisonous but also militates against the cardinal principles of classical liberalism. It is not surprising that educated people like Chidambaram and Aiyar, despite their admiration for America's economic system, end up condemning America. For they could not resist the meretricious charms of Leftist ideology.

12 How Intellectuals Spread Red Propaganda

More often than not, liberals act as the B-team of the commies, unquestioningly accepting their outlandish theories and slavishly spreading their propaganda.

When the National Democratic Alliance (NDA) government came to power under the Bharatiya Janata Party in 1998, Human Resource Development Minister Murli Manohar Joshi decided to take on the might of Marxist historians, who monopolized the writing of history textbooks. Joshi was pursuing his own narrow agenda of imposing Hindutva historiography, which is usually a queer mixture of sacred beliefs, saffron mythology, and shallow research.

Red historians started screaming, leveling all sorts of charges at Joshi, who soon became their favorite whipping boy. Our great intellectuals and liberals, like the sheep in Orwell's *Animal Farm*, faithfully echoed the communist lies. P. Chidambaram, Khushwant Singh, Kuldip Nayar, and other eminent intellectuals deplored Joshi for challenging Marxist academics. Among such intellectuals is Pankaj Mishra.

He has written a best-selling novel, *The Romantics*. He is an intellectual recognized in the West, regularly writing for important liberal publications such as *New York Times*. He helped globaliz-

ing the lies of Indian communists. In an article in 2001 in *New York Times*, he wrote:

> Murli Manohar Joshi promotes a new Indian history that highlights the depredations of Muslim invaders (as they are called) and celebrates Hindu bravery . . . . This sectarian-minded education is objected to by many of India's distinguished historians—especially those who had stressed India's pluralist traditions in their now discarded textbooks. Mr. Joshi recently denounced these historians as "academic terrorists" who were more difficult to fight than the usual kind of terrorist.

"India's distinguished historians" are undoubtedly "academic terrorists", for they terrorize anybody who dares to differ with them. If you do not fall in line, these "distinguished historians" would call you communal, fascist, bigoted, etc. Let's first see what "India's distinguished historians" have been writing. It must be noted here that their books were prescribed by the National Council of Educational Research & Training (NCERT) and were used for decades as standard textbooks. The council was dominated by Leftists; when their stranglehold was broken by Joshi, they let loose a barrage of abuse, calumny, and canards against the courageous minister. I will quote a few instances of blatant Leftwing bias in the writings of these pamphleteers who masquerade as academics.

Arjun Dev wrote the two-volume, *The Story of Civilization*, for class IX and class X. The book was prescribed during the 1970s, 1980s, and 1990s. In the chapter, "Socialist Movement and the Russian Revolution," he wrote:

> The October Revolution had been almost completely peaceful. Only two persons were reported killed in Petrograd on the day the Revolution took place. However, soon after the new state was involved in a civil war. The officers of the army of the fallen Czar organized an armed rebellion against the Soviet state.

Further, regarding the consequences of the Revolution:

> The overthrow of autocracy and the destruction of the aristocracy and the power of the Church were the first achievements of the Russian Revolution. The second was the building of the world's first socialist society. The Czarist empire was transformed into a new state called the Union of Soviet Socialist Republics (USSR). The policies of the new state were directed to the realization of the old socialist ideal, "from each according to his capacity, to each according to his work."
>
> Private property for production was abolished and the motive of private profit was eliminated from the system of production.
>
> The first task that the new government faced was the building up of a technologically advanced economy. To do this, a new procedure was adopted—economic planning. The industrial development of Europe in the 19th century had taken place as a result of the initiative of individual capitalists. In the USSR, industrialization was undertaken by the state, through the Five Year Plans. Under these plans, the entire resources of the economy were mobilized to attain an accelerated rate of economic development, keeping in view the purposes thereof—social and economic equality. The unprecedented rate of development in the USSR has demonstrated the effectiveness of planning as a means of progress.
>
> The Revolution resulted in the development of a new type of social and economic system in the USSR. By the abolition of private ownership and the profit motive, the existence of classes with mutually opposed interests was ended. Glaring inequalities in society disappeared.

In short, a paradise was created by the communists in a land benighted by the Czarist tyranny! What Dev does *not* mention are the odious aspects of this supposed heaven. In a typical Leftist fashion of hiding important facts, he blacks out the unprecedented violence unleashed by the Bolsheviks in Russia. The word "Cheka" does not figure anywhere in Dev's account; the student could not know about a vile secret organization, which was responsible for lakhs of deaths. As a leading historian Paul Johnson

wrote in *Modern Times*, "While the last Tsars had executed an average of seventeen a year (for all crimes), by 1918-19 the Cheka was averaging 1,000 executions a month for political offences alone." Another historian, an eye-witness, estimated that more than 50,000 death sentences were carried out by the Cheka by the end of 1920.

Further, Lenin added a new dimension to terrorism: the principle on which people were sentenced to death, says Johnson. According to Johnson:

> He [Lenin] was ceasing to be interested in *what* a man did or had done—let alone *why* he had done it—and was first encouraging, then commanding, his representative apparatus to hunt down people, and destroy them, not on the basis of crimes, real or imaginary, but on the basis of generalizations, hearsay, rumors. First came condemned categories: "prostitutes", "work-shirkers", "bagmen", "speculators", "hoarders", all of whom might vaguely be described as criminal. Following quickly, however, came entire occupational groups. The watershed was Lenin's decree of January 1918 calling on the agencies of the state to "purge the Russian land of all kinds of harmful insects". This was not a judicial act: it was an invitation to mass murder. Many years later, Alexander Sozhenitsyn listed just a few of the groups who included "former *zemstvo* members, people in the Cooper movements, homeowners, high-school teachers, parish councils and choirs, priests, monks and nuns, Tolstoyan pacifists, officials of trade unions"—soon to classified as "former people". Quite quickly the condemned group decree-laws extended to whole classes and the notion of killing people collectively rather than individually was seized upon by the Cheka professionals with enthusiasm.

Some "collectivization" to end "glaring inequalities in society"!

But our distinguished historian, Dev, does not see all this. Nor does he see any oppression or repression of the non-Russian nationalities. He wrote: "On the question of non-Russian nationalities Bolsheviks were the only party with a clear policy. Lenin had described the Russian empire as a 'prison of nations' and had de-

clared that no genuine democracy could be established unless all the non-Russian peoples were given equal rights. He had proclaimed the right of all peoples to self-determination, including those under the Russian empire." So, after the Revolution, "the equality of the nationalities comprising the USSR was given legal form in the constitution drafted in 1923 and later under the 1935 constitution. Equal representation was assured to all the nationalities in one of the two chambers of the USSR legislature. The republics formed by these nationalities were allowed considerable autonomy which facilitated the development of their languages and cultures. These areas were far more backward economically than European Russia, but through planned economic development and the spread of education, they were soon modernized."

The *Encyclopedia Britannica*, however, has a different story to tell: "Neither before nor after the Russian Revolution of 1917 were the nationalist aspirations of the Muslims of Central Asia compatible with the interests of the Russian state or those of the European population of the region. This was demonstrated once and for all when the troops of the Tashkent Soviet crushed a short-lived Muslim government established in Kokand in January 1918." Once good sense dawned on the ruling class in Moscow, and it loosened its stranglehold over the central Asian republics, all of them opted for independence—giving a lie to the assertions of Dev and other Marxist historians. Ditto with the Caucasian and Baltic republics, and the satellite states of the USSR in eastern Europe.

Let's move on to another distinguished historian, Satish Chandra, whose two-volume *Medieval India* is prescribed by the NCERT for the students of class XI and XII. Satish Chandra and others of his ilk have been comprehensively exposed in Arun Shourie's *Eminent Historians*. Shourie has shown how Chandra denigrated Hinduism, reducing it to an abomination called Brahminism, which amounts to the exploitation and oppression of lower caste people. "By contrast," writes Shourie, "the aggression, the butchery, the devastations committed by Islamic rulers are sanitized through a three-layered filter. First, the devastation is

attributed to individuals and not the religion. Among individuals, it is made out that just a few individuals—a few isolated exceptions—indulged in it. Third, that they committed aggression, destroyed temples, pulverized idols, not because of some religious belief but because, being rulers, they had to put down their opponents who happened to be Hindus; and because they were motivated by mundane considerations like greed for the riches of temples, the need to establish political sway over the conquered territory, etc."

The liberals—and their intellectual mentors, the Leftists—abuse Shourie as a communal, fascist writer. However, what he has written is incontrovertible. He has quoted from the accounts of historians and chroniclers of the medieval period (relying on Sita Ram Goel's path-breaking *Hindu Temples: What Happened to Them*), who not only faithfully recounted the depredations of Islam but also rejoiced in them. This despite the fact that the accounts of Ziaud-din Barani, Shamsu'd-din bin Siraju'd-din, Ferishta, and others are considered authentic sources of information by Satish Chandra himself. One of the sultans, Firuz Shah Tughlaq, wrote a book in which he boasted of destroying temples. Yet, Chandra insists that the sultans followed a "policy of broad toleration"! In fact, it has been a sustained endeavor of Chandra to negate, ignore, or gloss over the massacres carried out by Muslim rulers—that is, to misinform and mislead the student.

Finally, we examine the case of Bipan Chandra, whose *Modern India* was prescribed by the NCERT for the students of class XI and XII. He is a master of equivocation and prevarication; he would cite an exception as a law, and vice-versa. Well, all Left-wing intellectuals do that, but it is only a few who excel in such shenanigans; Bipan Chandra is one of those few. He wrote:

> Socialist and Communist groups came into existence in the 1920s. The example of the Russian Revolution had aroused interest among many young nationalists. Many of them were dissatisfied with Gandhian political ideas and programmes and turned to socialist ideology for guidance. M.N. Roy became the first Indian to be elected to the leadership of the Communist In-

ternational. In 1924, the government arrested Muzaffar Ahmed and S.A. Dange, accused them of spreading Communist ideas, and tried them along with others in the Kanpur Conspiracy case. In 1925, the Communist Party [of India] came into existence. Moreover, many worker and peasant parties were founded in different pats of the country. These parties and groups propagated Marxist and communist ideas. At the same time, they remained integral parts of the national movement and the National Congress.

Notice in what glowing terms our distinguished historian has described the communists and the grand role socialism played in guiding the national movement. Notice also the mendacity of the historian who eulogizes M.N. Roy for his achievement of getting elected to the leadership of the Comintern—for whatever it is worth of; but refuses to mention a word about the insincerity and embezzlements of Roy's. This despite the fact even communists have accused Roy of misappropriation of funds.

Reading the above passage, one may get the impression that in the 1920s pro-Marxist worker and peasant parties—which remained "integral parts of the national movement and the National Congress"—formed the matrix of the freedom struggle; that the Communist Party was a force to reckon with; that Marxist ideas and ideals played a great and glorious role in the national movement. However, Saumyendranath Tagore, a leader of the Bengal Workers' and Peasants Party, went to Moscow in 1927 and told the Comintern leadership that "the actual number of communists in India . . . did not exceed more than a dozen . . . ." This is also corroborated by J.N. Sahni, a journalist who wrote in his memoirs, *The Lid Off*, that communists were of no consequence till the British decided to prosecute them in the Meerut Conspiracy case (1929-33). In fact, it was after Mahatma Gandhi expressed his sympathy for communists that people became aware of their existence. It is another matter that the communists were abusing Gandhiji as "the evil pacifist genius", equating him with Judas. Further, Bipan Chandra does not write a word about the traitorous role played by the communists in 1942, when not merely did they

not participate in the Quit India Movement but actually helped the British.

Bipan Chandra does not merely negate and conceal the misdemeanors and misdeeds of communists; when it comes to writing about Muslims, he again indulges in prevarication and evasion. According to him, "in Malabar (northern Kerala), the Moplahs, or Muslim peasants, created a powerful anti-zamindar movement." Some gloss! A violent Islamist movement becomes "a powerful anti-zamindar movement". This is Marxian historiography at its extreme: since the Theory does not recognize any factor other than economic, even Islamic terror is explained in economic terms.

Needless to say, Bipan Chandra is lying on the Moplah massacres; even Mahatma Gandhi, one of the greatest champions of Hindu-Muslim unity, considered Moplah violence a blow to communal harmony.

I can cite myriad examples of the insincerity and mendacity the so-called distinguished historians. All of them—Romila Thapar, R.S. Sharma, D.N. Jha—distort truths and spread lies. It is impossible to gauge the damage they have inflicted upon the society, by vending dangerous lies. What is worse is that liberals and intellectuals like Pankaj Mishra accept without question the authenticity and the authority of such "distinguished historians".

13 The Descendants of Gandhari

Some are born blind, some get afflicted with blindness, and some blindfold themselves. Communists belong to the first category; liberals and intellectuals belong to the other two categories. Communists are blind in the sense that they cannot see the world as it exists; worse, they do not *want* to see the world as it exists. In any case, their world came to an end with the collapse of the Soviet Union, the fall of Berlin Wall, and the adoption free market by China and Third World nations. American conservative author Gerhart Niemeyer wrote in 1963 in *The Communist Mind:*

> Communists have put between themselves and all other people a deliberate and profound alienation, or estrangement. They postulate that all who have not cast their will and thought into the communist mold of the socialist future cannot live in the same world with communists. Communists cannot and will not accept the world in which, on their showing, all non-communists actually live. Thus their design with respect to these other people is to remake them into the communist image.

Communists have clearly failed; but they have not taken their failing gracefully, or even accepted that they have failed; they have, instead, become schizophrenic. The communists of West Bengal are a good example: those running the state government often go by the precepts and practices of free market economics; their comrades in New Delhi and in the trade union movement

continue to spew venomous radicalism. Perhaps, the communist movement in India will follow the Chinese example: embrace market while lauding socialism.

Liberals and intellectuals continue to build ivory towers, which have been rendered grotesque by the architecture of postmodernism. Excessive exposure to Marxian philosophy has not only blinded them but also made them unfit to live outside their hermitages. Such exposure has given them the impression that world outside is essentially unjust, unfair, and inequitable; for socialism has failed and capitalism is on ascendance; and, in their scheme of things, socialism is good and capitalism is bad. And the world is going from bad to worse, since it has turned its back on socialism. Needless to say, their assumptions and axioms are false and misleading, but they do not want to have a hard look at their assumptions. It took the courage of a Copernicus to challenge received wisdom, resulting in repudiation of age-old theories about astronomy and opening up of new vistas of knowledge and learning. Another "Copernican revolution" was effected by Immaneul Kant when he, in his own words, was aroused from his "dogmatic slumbers" by David Hume. But our academics and scholars are neither Copernicus nor Kant; they refuse to step out of the ivory towers of pedantry and political correctness; they are afraid of the real world and its disturbing realities. Ensconced in their campuses and seminar halls, they keep lambasting the world because it fails to conform to their theories and fantasies.

Yet, these worthies are not without consequence, whether in India or in the US. Their sway over academia and academics is undiminished, though not unchallenged. In India, former Human Resources Development Minister Murli Manohar Joshi made a heroic, though unsuccessful, effort to challenge the Leftwing mafia which rules universities and educational institutions. In the US, however, the conservatives were able to set up an entire counter-establishment, to challenge the received wisdom of the East Coast liberals.

Liberals and intellectuals do not lack the faculty of seeing; they just do not want to see things—especially evil—as they are; and

for this reason, they blindfold themselves. They are the descendants of Gandhari.

In *Mahabharata*, Gandhari was the queen of Dhritrashtra, who was born blind. As a token of loyalty to her husband, she decided to blindfold herself. Dhritrashtra was blind not only literally but also figuratively: he could not see the evil deeds of his sons Duryodhan and Duhshashan. But Gandhari's blindness was not less profound: she *chose* not to see the misdemeanors of her sons.

The liberals and intellectuals of our age are the descendants of Gandhari because they *choose* not to see evil, wherever and in whichever form it may exist. They have played an extremely negative role in modern times; in the contemporary era, their words and deeds have become even more dangerous, for the communists are seen as fossils and few have the time or patience to trudge through the labyrinthine passages of postmodernism that Leftwing intellectuals love to build.

Let's begin our discourse on the self-imposed blindness of liberals and intellectuals with a glimpse of the global scene. In his *Modern Times*, the historian Paul Johnson wrote about reaction of Western liberals to Stalinist brutalities:

> In the outside world, the magnitude of the Stalin tyranny—or indeed its very existence—was scarcely grasped at all. Most of those who traveled to Russia were either businessmen, anxious to trade and with no desire to probe or criticize what did not concern them, or intellectuals who came to admire and, still more, to believe. If the decline of Christianity created the modern political zealot—and his crimes—so the evaporation of religious faith among the educated left a vacuum in the minds of Western intellectuals easily filled by secular superstitions. There is not other explanation for the credulity with which scientists, accustomed to evaluating evidence, and writers, whose whole function was to study and criticize society, accepted the crudest Stalinist propaganda at its face value. They *needed* to believe; they *wanted* to be duped. [emphasis added]

For such worthies, the Soviet Union was their pilgrimage—you don't go on pilgrimage with a questioning mind. When the devout Hindu doctors, engineers, and scientists go to the Kumbh, they *know* that the Ganges is polluted and yet they take the dip. So, Sidney and Beatrice Webb lauded a project built with slave labor. Harold Laski praised Soviet prisons for enabling convicts to lead "a full and self-respecting life". George Bernard Shaw compared British jails, where a human being is transformed into a criminal, with Russian prisons where a man entered "as a criminal type and would come out an ordinary man but for the difficulty of inducing him to come out at all. As far as I could make out they could stay as long as they liked it". This about the most horrendous slave camps mankind has ever witnessed!

The mendacity of Leftist intellectuals and liberals was unbounded. According to Johnson:

> The famine of 1932, the worst in Russian history, was virtually unreported. At the height of it, the visiting biologist Julian Huxley found "a level of physique and general health rather above that to be seen in England." Shaw threw his food supplies out of the train window just before crossing the Russian frontier "convinced that there were no shortages in Russia" . . . .
>
> Estimates of Stalin written in the years 1929-34 make curious reading. H.G. Wells said he had "never met a man more candid, fair and honest . . . no one is afraid of him and everybody trusts him." The Webbs argued that he had less power than an American president and was merely acting on the orders of the Central Committee and the Presidium . . . . He [Stalin] was, said the Chilean writer Pablo Neruda, "a good-natured man of principle" . . . .
>
> . . . Self-delusion was obviously the biggest single factor in the presentation of an unsuccessful despotism as a Utopia in the making. But there was also conscious deception by men and women who thought of themselves as idealists and who, at the time, honestly believed they were serving a higher human purpose by systematic misrepresentation and lying. If the Great War with its unprecedented violence brutalized the world, the Great Depression corrupted it by appearing to limit the options before

> humanity and presenting them in garishly contrasting terms. Political activists felt they had to make terrible choices and, having made them, stick to them with desperate resolution. The Thirties was the age of the heroic lie. Saintly mendacity became its more prized virtue. Stalin's tortured Russia was the prime beneficiary of this sanctified falsification. The competition to deceive became more fierce when Stalinism acquired a moral rival in Hitler's Germany.

The Western intellectual has lived his "heroic" lies with aplomb, but his Indian counterpart is not far behind. As we saw in chapter after chapter in this book, he can give the Western intellectual a run for his money when it comes to "heroic" lies and "saintly mendacity".

While during the Cold War era the mendacity was about veiling the ugly face of communism, in the 21st century the mission is to downplay Islamic terror. There is no dearth of liberals, intellectuals, and politicians in the West who gloss over the fanaticism, aggression, and illiberality of Islam (see the chapter on Islam), which Islamic terrorists use to motivate their cohorts and justify their acts of terrorism. The best-selling author Karen Armstrong, academic Edward Said, linguist-polemicist Noam Chomsky, and former US President Bill Clinton are some such apologists of Islam. Their Indian counterparts are the Khushwant Singhs and Kuldip Nayars, the Rafiq Zakarias and Mushirul Hasans, the Mani Shankar Aiyars and P. Chidambarams, the Arundhati Roys and Pankaj Mishras. These worthies are some of the most illustrious peddlers of falsehoods and half-truths; there are many others peddlers, often less celebrated, but no less dangerous in spreading lies and deceit, in further disfiguring the already perverted public discourse—in spreading darkness and promoting blindness.

Unlike communists, the Indian liberals and intellectuals do not consider the world essentially evil. But they do not question the basic premises and postulates of the Left; often, they blindly accept Leftist theories as self-evident truths, and end up mouthing outdated shibboleths. The result is: the blind leading the blindfolded.

The blind leading the blindfolded was the greatest pathology of the twentieth century, as more than 100 million died under various communist regimes. It would be smug optimism to assume that all maladies of the past have been taken care of.

14 Guilt
Weapon of Mass Deception

While discussing assault strategy, military commanders use a term called "softening the target". It connotes actions that facilitate the capture of a post, bunker, or any other target. The actions can be bombardment by the air force aircraft or heavy shelling by artillery; both were used by India in its war with Pakistan in Kargil in 1999. Aerial and territorial bombardment softens up the target by causing destruction and engendering disarray in the enemy camp, thus making the task of the infantry less dangerous.

Communists and Leftwing authors perform the task of softening the target: their target is civilization; they want to destroy it. And their weapon—the weapon of mass deception—is collective guilt. Communists have for long yearned to mold human civilization as per their dogmas—dialectical materialism, scientific socialism, etc. Such has been their spell over mankind in the twentieth century that even the most erudite and brilliant leaders—Jawaharlal Nehru being a prime example—got besotted by the perversion called communism. It is another matter that wherever communism succeeded, it left a trail of unprecedented gore, devastation, and despair. More than 100 million perished under various socialist regimes in the last century. According to Jung Chung and Jon Halliday, authors of *Mao: The Unknown Story*

(October 2005), the Great Helmsman's barbarity alone was responsible for the killing of about 70 million people.

An equally disturbing fact is that despite all their crimes, communists—at least in India—are seldom accused of having done anything wrong. They always adopt a holier-than-thou posture on any and every issue; they masquerade as the champions of the poor, defenders of pluralism, *avante-garde* of enlightenment, and flag-bearers of modernity and humanism.

Having failed to win the world for their cause, communists have instead sought to destroy what exists. That is, they want to destroy liberal democracy, market economy, individual freedom, open society: they want to destroy human civilization.

Communists and Leftwing authors perform the dual task: one, of deflecting the attention of society from their own misdemeanors; and two, of shifting blame to others. Doing so, they use guilt, among other things, to seek acceptance and legitimacy in a civilized society. Usually, they succeed, as guilt is, in the words of historian Paul Johnson, "the corrosive vice of the civilized." Where does this vice come from?

From the human nature.

There seems to be some merit in Immanuel Kant's ethical theory, which emphasizes the absoluteness and universal validity of morals. The great eighteenth century philosopher wrote, "So act as to treat humanity in your own person or in that of any other, in every case as an end and never as merely a means only." It hurts when we see our follow beings in misery and agony: as victims of natural calamities like floods, earthquakes, or tsunami; as casualties in wars and violent ethnic conflicts; as the poor suffering from all sorts of adversities. We feel compassion, which often becomes the thin edge of the wedge to spread the feeling of collective guilt.

Reds and intellectuals use compassion to drill guilt into the hearts and minds of the civilized. Therefore, most man-made ills are attributed to one or the other defining feature or consummate fruit of civilization, be it capitalism, globalization, Western civilization, or Hinduism. Hence the guilt of capitalism: heartless treatment of children in the days of Charles Dickens, miserable

conditions of workers in the nineteenth century England, etc. And the guilt of globalization: whether it is the Asian crisis of 1997 or socio-economic problems in any poor country in the world, it is globalization that is blamed for causing or worsening them. And Western guilt: oppression and exploitation of Asian and African nations, bad treatment of original inhabitants of the Americas and Australia, etc. And Hindu guilt: severity against the Shudras, as the lower caste people were called, over the centuries, the rigid caste system, the subjugation of women, and so on.

I'll begin with a couple of anecdotes, illustrating how guilt, which has entered our psyche, finds expression in facile analysis and everyday conversation. The first one is from a chapter of *Open Secrets: India's Intelligence Unveiled* by Maloy Krishna Dhar, former joint director of Intelligence Bureau. It is one of the most controversial books published in India (2005) in recent times—controversial because of its disclosures regarding the misuse of official intelligence apparatus by politicians in power.

Dhar, an Indian Police Service (IPS) officer of the 1964 batch, got the West Bengal cadre. In his early years of career, he was posted at Naxalbari in West Bengal, the cradle of the violent communist movement in India. It is a well-known fact that the Naxals, as the adherents of the movement came to be called, were traitors; their allegiance was to Beijing and their slogan was "China's chairman is our chairman". So, what was the reaction of India's rulers? One would have expected the entire political class to unite and support the armed forces in their fight against the Naxals. But what actually happened? "To Delhi Naxalbari rumblings were insignificant sparks and the ruling Communist and Bangla Congress leaders conjured up a suicidal policy of destroying the very constitutional, political and administrative edifices, which they were supposed to uphold," writes Dhar.

A group led by the local Naxal leader, Jangal Santhal, "drew first police blood near Kheru Jote when a police party headed by inspector Sonam Wangdi was ambushed . . . . Wangdi was a fine investigating officer, but did not have training in facing an armed hostile mob. The cult of armed mob violence by ideologically

maddened cadres was new to the police force in West Bengal." In fact, it was new to the entire nation. A few battalions of the Eastern Frontier Rifles and the State Armed Police were no doubt inducted. Dhar continues:

> But other highly visible and unusual forces too descended on Naxalbari to supervise the police action. Senior ministers like Harekrishan Konar and Sushil Dhara, etc. camped in the police state to shoulder the responsibility of guiding the police operations in accordance with their brand of ideological policing. With the ministers around the top revenue and police administration officials too converged on the tiny town. The ministers had laid down new policing norms: wait and watch and to see that "legal violence" was not applied against the "Naxals," who attacked human lives and plundered properties with impunity. Left to the district administration the "law and order" aspects of the movement could have been taken care of within a few weeks. But the ideologically fired ministers of the government wanted to usher in "people's democracy" add new dimensions to the concept of destroying the constitutional order from within and chase a chimera called social revolution through the tools of anarchy and class annihilation . . .
>
> It was abundantly made clear that I should not use force without explicit permission of the ministers camping in the police station.

Dhar points out that the Naxals were a murderous and intolerant lot. They killed Jagadananda Roy, a Left-leaning revolutionary who had fought against the British Empire. The young police officer successfully aborted a violent Naxal attack on the house of a farmer. In this encounter, a few members of Jangal Santhal's "revolutionary army" were injured. The reward? One of the camping ministers, Konar who was a Marxist, threatened Dhar with dismissal!

The ministers were not Naxals; in fact, the Naxals were baying for their blood. Yet, they were sympathetic towards the violent extremists. The cause of their sympathy towards the Naxalbari

movement was guilt—the guilt of not being able to ameliorate the conditions of poor peasants, sharecroppers, and tribals; the guilt of not being socialistic enough so as to usher in an egalitarian paradise on earth. And here lies the irony and the tragedy of contemporary India. The irony: socialism is the system that impedes economic growth and development, the system that curtails the eradication of poverty, the system that empowers the politician and the bureaucrat; and yet in India the cure for socialism is sought not in its abolition but in *more* socialism. The tragedy: the nation is not able to get rid of socialism lock, stock, and barrel. Meanwhile guilt pervades further, permeating the public debate, infecting the body-politic, dominating the minds and hearts of those who matter.

What is worse is that even those who suffer from the hands of Naxals are guilt-ridden. Dhar, for instance, perceives Naxalism as "an idea that provides courage and tools to the have-nots to fight for their rights"! The observation is not merely trite; it betrays the blind acceptance and internalization of the Leftwing proposition: unjust social and economic conditions are responsible for terrorism, insurgency, or revolutionary violence. The truth is that Naxalism, like other forms of terrorism, does not have much to do with socio-economic conditions or poverty. In fact, there is little correlation between poverty and revolutionary violence. The French Revolution, for instance, did not happen because the incidence of poverty, repression, and oppression was the worst over there; in 1789, in most countries of the world the condition of the poor was much worse than that of the French peasants; yet, there was a revolution in France. Closer home, there was insurgency in Punjab for more than a decade; there is still terrorism in Kashmir. This despite the fact that the two are among better-off states of India. But Dhar continues to parrot the supposed relationship between poverty and terrorism.

The second anecdote about the spread of guilt is from my first-hand experience. At a party in the fall of 2005, I was talking to a distant relative. A retired colonel from the Indian Army, he is employed as security in-charge of a medium-sized company near

Delhi. He was talking about the company he worked with, his job profile, his interaction with workers, the union leaders, and so on. Then he said something that baffled me: "Sometimes, I feel guilty for being part of a system that exploits poor workers." Does his company not pay the employees the minimum wages, as stipulated by the authorities, I asked him. It does pay them, he answered. Then where is the exploitation, I asked. The conversation ended abruptly as some of his acquaintances wanted to talk to him, but I kept thinking about it.

Here was a man who has served in the most British institution of the country, the Indian Army—an institution that has largely escaped the dangerous enthusiasms of our politicians, the imbecilic fads of social justice, the rabidity of social engineering. And yet he is mouthing a shibboleth—that big companies exploit workers, that market economy is essentially exploitative—that has been comprehensively and indubitably proven wrong. As we saw in the chapter on Jawaharlal Nehru, capitalism or market economy is the only system in which there is *no* exploitation.

So we find two gentlemen, a seasoned cop and a senior army official, resonating Leftist ideas. It shows the pervasiveness and preponderance of Leftist ideas. This has become possible because of the intellectual influence of the Left, an influence that is greatly disproportionate to its political strength. The education system, academia, the media, the entire opinion-making apparatus—everything has been monopolized by the commies and pinkish intellectuals. They distort history to indoctrinate the young, impressionable minds as per their convenience. Anybody who challenges the intellectual mafia—as former Human Resources Development Minister Murli Manohar Joshi did—is demonized, denounced, and derided. The Leftist mafia has many tools and techniques in its repertory—slander, falsification, sophistry, sanctimoniousness, disingenuousness, guilt-mongering. The last one is most widely used.

In India, more than half a century of guilt-mongering and other Leftist tricks has created a climate of opinion in which Marxist lies pass off as gospel truth. By the way, guilt-mongering is a lucrative

industry in the West as well. But in Western countries, especially in the US, there is a vigorous Rightwing movement to counter and debunk Leftist lies. In the US, for instance, black conservative author Thomas Sowell has steadfastly written against the purveyors of guilt. He has consistently attacked the liberal establishment that continues to pontificate over white racism and the explains all black problems as the "legacy of slavery." He comes out with facts that would astonish any educated person. According to him, Islamic societies enslaved more Africans than Europeans did. Sowell points out that this fact is ignored and sole emphasis is laid on European enslavement of Africa. The idea is "to score ideological points against American society or Western civilization, or to induce guilt and thereby extract benefits from the white population today". This is truer in India than in the West; our history books, particularly those written by commies, are testimony to that; Bipan Chandra, the Don Corleone of History Mafia, has also been involved in distorting, among other things, the history of slavery.

In an article on February 8, 2005, Sowell wrote:

> It seems so obvious today that, as Lincoln said, if slavery is not wrong, then nothing is wrong. But no country anywhere believed that three centuries ago.
>
> A very readable and remarkable new book that has just been published—*Bury the Chains* by Adam Hochschild—traces the history of the world's first anti-slavery movement, which began with a meeting of 12 "deeply religious" men in London in 1787.
>
> The book re-creates the very different world of that time, in which slavery was so much taken for granted that most people simply did not think about it, one way or the other. Nor did the leading intellectuals, political leaders, or religious leaders in Britain or anywhere else in the world.
>
> The dozen men who formed the world's first anti-slavery movement saw their task as getting their fellow Englishmen to think about slavery—about the brutal facts and about the moral implications of those facts.

> Their conviction that this would be enough to turn the British public, and ultimately the British Empire, against slavery might seem naive, except that this is precisely what happened. It did not happen quickly and it did not happen without encountering bitter opposition, for the British were at the time the world's biggest slave traders and this created wealthy and politically powerful special interests defending slavery.
>
> The anti-slavery movement nevertheless persisted through decades of struggles and defeats in Parliament until eventually they secured a ban on the international slave trade, and ultimately a ban on slavery itself throughout the British Empire.
>
> Even more remarkable, Britain took it upon itself, as the leading naval power of the world, to police the ban on slave trading against other nations. Intercepting and boarding other countries' ships on the high seas to look for slaves, the British became and remained for more than a century the world's policeman when it came to stopping the slave trade . . .
>
> Chances do not look good. The anti-slavery movement was spearheaded by people who would today be called "the religious right" and its organization was created by conservative businessmen. Moreover, what destroyed slavery in the non-Western world was Western imperialism.
>
> Nothing could be more jolting and discordant with the vision of today's intellectuals than the fact that it was businessmen, devout religious leaders and Western imperialists who together destroyed slavery around the world. And if it doesn't fit their vision, it is the same to them as if it never happened.

Such facts do not fit into the Left's scheme of things; so, they are either ignored or downplayed. Hence the emphasis on white guilt. And Western guilt. And capitalist guilt. And Hindu guilt. But, as V.S. Naipaul asked in an interview, where is Arab guilt (regarding Arabs' role in slavery)? One may ask many similar questions: Where is Muslim guilt (regarding ill-treatment of women, non-Muslims, etc.)? Where is socialist guilt (economic devastation in countries like India)? Where is communist guilt (killing of millions of people in China, Soviet Union, Cambodia,

etc)? No answers. The attempt is to suppress facts, but the truth, and promote a kingdom of mendacity.

Communists and Leftwing intellectuals are the generals of the kingdom of mendacity. Human civilization is the target; they are softening the target by using the strategy of guilt-mongering. The bombardment of lies and white lies continues unabated. More often than not, liberals end up as accomplices of the Left in this war against civilization. They become useful for the commies. That is why Lenin called them "useful idiots".

15 The Way Out
Indian Right

Is Indian Right possible? In India it is the members of Sangh Parivar who could be vaguely called Rightwing or conservative. But only *vaguely*; for often they are dangerously close to the Left; and sometimes they are definitively anti-conservative.

It is pertinent to mention here that by conservatism I mean a political philosophy. Unfortunately, the terms Rightwing and "conservative" are considered synonymous—more so in India than in the West—with illiberal, orthodox, unchanging, regressive, fogy, unimaginative, etc. Typically, a conservative would be regarded as somebody who does not allow his wife to come out of the *purdah*, doesn't send his daughter to school, is not comfortable with modern ways of life, and is generally a nasty person. As a political philosophy, conservatism is something very different.

The three strands of conservatism in the West are: open society, free economy, and limited government. Not that conservatism is a well-defined system, with established dogmas (*a la* dialectical materialism of Marxism) and universal doctrines; there are numerous variations in the conservative theme; besides, conservative beliefs have grown over the centuries. Yet, in almost every variety of conservatism, the three strands of open society, free economy, and limited government are always present. And individual liberty

is always a cornerstone of conservatism, though liberty is located in the concrete reality of society rather than in some abstraction.

It may be argued that conservatism is a quintessentially Western phenomenon, that it is the child of Anglo-Scottish Enlightenment, that it is relevant only in the Anglo-Saxon world or, at the most, for the Western civilization. While it is true that conservatism first took a concrete shape in the works of philosophers such as Adam Smith, David Hume, and Edmund Burke—and has grown as a leading political philosophy primarily in the Anglo-Saxon world—our contention is that Rightwing or conservatism *is* possible in India. Of course, Indian conservatism has to be home-grown, arising from and in tune with the conventions and traditions of the country. It is possible because India is an ancient civilization; it can boast of a society that is sufficiently vibrant and resilient, readily absorbing Western values without losing its cultural moorings, as evident from the experience of the last two centuries.

The chasm between the Orient and the Occident is not as wide as it is made out to be; nor are the difference so huge that would restrict the relevance of a political philosophy to only one part of the world. At any rate, questions of universal relevance were seldom raised when, at one point or the other, serious attempts were made to implant communism, which is indubitably of Western origin, in countries as diverse as India, China, Vietnam, Cuba, and Zimbabwe.

Also, conservatism is not entirely unknown to the Orient. Japan, the only Asian country in the G-8 club, has considerable experience in conservatism. According to *Encyclopedia Britannica*:

> Except for the period of intervention by the militarists during the 1930s and 1940s, Japan has been ruled by conservatives since the beginning of party politics in the 1880s . . . .
>
> The Liberal-Democratic Party [which is conservative] is intimately linked with big business interests, and its policies are guided primarily by the objective of fostering a stable environment for the development of Japan's free-enterprise economy; to this end, the party functions as a broker of conflicting business

interests. Policy toward other Asian countries, national defense, and internal security are other conservative preoccupations.

Conservatism has clearly worked in Japan—at least, it has worked better than militarism.

As for India, conservatism is not only possible but also *necessary*—necessary to tap the boundless potential of the people, necessary to liberate them from the clutches of a predatory and egregious political class, necessary for full emancipation of the economy; for Indian society is much healthier than the Indian state; and, one may add, the Indian people are much worthier than their politicians. The answer is conservatism.

Our contention is that open society, free economy, and limited government are not just the three strands of conservatism but they are so intertwined that it is impossible to separate any of them and yet not tamper with the whole. Let's begin with free market and open society. Adam Smith is known for propounding the virtues of the free market; but there is more to Smith than the doctrine of invisible hand. For Smith, *laissez-faire* capitalism was not just an economic system in which prices and wages got adjusted; it was a system of perfect liberty. As Fredrick Hayek wrote, Smith shared with David Hume and other Scottish philosophers an insight that "enabled them for the first time to comprehend how institutions and morals, language and law, have evolved by a process of cumulative growth and that it is only with and within this framework that human reason has grown and can successfully operate. Their argument is directed throughout against the Cartesian conception of an independently and antecedently existing human that invented these institutions and against the conception of civil society [that] was formed by some wise original legislator or an original 'social contract'. The latter idea of intelligent men coming together for deliberation about how to make the world anew is perhaps the most characteristic feature of those design theories."

In other words, there is also an invisible hand, so to speak, that operates in society. As Hayek puts it, our society, language, morals, etc, are the result of human *action* but not of human *design*. So the best possible course for a conservative philosophy would be to

let the invisible hand do its work in society; for that, we should respect the traditions and conventions, providing them the necessary autonomy. And we should be cautious against any endeavor in the direction of "social engineering".

Many members of the Sangh Parivar believe that it is possible to adopt the economic philosophy of the Left and wed it to their own "cultural nationalism". What these worthies do not realize is the fact that the economic philosophy of the Left is predicated on the principle that is antithetical to the very foundation of the Parivar's ideology: that Indian society is essentially sick and rotten, which cannot be cured without medication or surgery by the State. That is why all Leftists, pinkish intellectuals, and Left-libbers keep crying about State intervention in society and economy—more reservations for women and "weaker sections" in government and now also in the private sector. They keep denigrating Hindu society for all its real and imaginary sins. If some alien were to land on earth and come across only a few Indian Leftist publications, he would conclude that Hindu society is the most rigid, superstitious, stupid, iniquitous, unfair, and cruel; here bride-burning is a favorite urban pastime; and in remote areas, dalits are routinely massacred and women are frequently forced to become suttee.

The fact, however, is that the State is sick and rotten; governance has become a joke. Fortunately, there are people in all political parties, spread all over the ideological spectrum, who realize that the state's sickness is beyond redemption; so, they are trying to rollback the state, thus opening up opportunities for citizens. This is all what liberalization and privatization are all about. Arun Shourie calls it "consensus in practice"; it can also be seen as "conservatism in practice".

Peter Viereck wrote in the entry on conservatism in *Encyclopedia Britannica*, "Liberalism argues; conservatism simply *is*. When conservatism becomes ideologized, logical, and self-conscious, then it resembles the liberal rationalism that it opposes . . . . Whereas the liberal and rationalist mind consciously articulates abstract blueprints, the conservative mind unconsciously incarnates concrete traditions. And, because conservatism embodies

rather than argues, its best insights are almost never developed into sustained theoretical works equal to those of liberalism and radicalism."

In Great Britain and the United States, the conservatives can afford to "unconsciously" incarnate "concrete traditions"—though, fortunately, they don't do that—since the basic instinct in the Anglo-Saxon world is conservative. Interestingly, as we shall see later, it is in India that "conservatism simply *is*". And it is in India that there is a need to develop conservatism or some kind of Rightwing ideology. If this is not done, wherever the conservative attitude does exist, it would be swallowed by Leftist philosophy. The process has already started: many leaders of the Sangh Parivar champion the cause of social engineering, a concept that gnaws at the heart of any conservative or nationalist ideology; BJP leaders keep coming up with reservation schemes based on caste, thus implicitly accepting the Leftist charge that Hindu society is unjust, unfair, and iniquitous. In other words, the economic philosophy of genuine Indian conservatism *has to be* anti-Left.

Though most conservatives would agree on leaving the market to fend for itself or rely on the invisible hand for corrections, a number of conservatives—especially, the neo-conservatives like Irving Kristol—would argue that society cannot be given that kind of liberty. In his celebrated essay, *Pornography, Obscenity, and the Case for Censorship*, Kristol wrote:

> The purpose of any political regime is to achieve some version of the good life and the good society. It is not at all difficult to imagine a perfectly functioning democracy which answers all questions except one—why should anyone of intelligence and spirit care a fig for it?

People in every society do envision "the good life and the good society"; but it is done unconsciously, as unconsciously as the conservative mind "incarnates concrete traditions". But should it be the "purpose of any political regime" to achieve such version of the good life and the good society? And can there ever be a consensus on the means to achieve such version? Would it not lead to

some or other sort of social engineering? In fact, such an endeavor would be a threat to the open society, in the present as well as in the future. No matter what is the nature of this endeavor, Rightist or Leftist, the results are always disastrous.

Let's see what a Rightist vision does. Former Information & Broadcasting Minister Sushma Swaraj wants to guard our morals, as also the glorious Hindu culture against the onslaught of the decadent Western culture. She was responsible for taking many a TV advertisement off the air as they threatened to "pollute our culture" (whatever that means). She also launched a campaign against Fashion TV, the channel devoted to fashion trends. Given a chance, she would become the Big Sister, deciding what women should wear and men should watch, what people should do when they freak out; she would like to be the Minister for the Promotion of Virtue and Abolition of Vice, on the lines of Taliban. What is her vision? It is of a society in which women wear *sarees* (and, if they are married, also apply a huge *bindi* and copious amount of vermilion on their forehead); men devote their life for the greater glory of the nation. In general, men and women lead a spiritual life, have sex (strictly in missionary position) only to produce children, raise them in a sanitized environment, free from decadent Western influences. People should maintain moral hygiene. This is the saffron universe the lady minister wants to create. This, she believes, will make her a champion of Indian culture; such posturing will also help the BJP catch votes. Apparently, she feels that she is echoing the sentiments of Hindus, who are supposedly offended by the abominations like *The Bold & The Beautiful* and *Baywatch*. The vision is, in fact, the conventional wisdom which, in this case, is a product and function of the classic myth of Eastern Spiritualism-Western Materialism. Swaraj makes Hinduism look dull and bland, retrograde and authoritarian—a saffron version of Marxian totalitarianism in which the entire society, along with polity, economy, arts, and culture, is controlled and regimented. Unfortunately, she is not alone in the Sangh Parivar championing such regimentation. Unless checked vigorously, the Sanghis will start coming up with more and more stupid diktats:

what to wear, which movies to watch, which ads and serials to ban, which books to prescribe and which ones to proscribe, and so on—they will continue to sermonize on each and every such issue. And they would leave no stone unturned to effect their sermons. The saffron brigade feels bad when young men and women exchange cards on Valentine's Day; they don't have compunctions in physically assaulting young couples who celebrate Valentine's Day. The brigade is the enemy of open society.

The saffron brigade does not recognize the fact that a most important factor responsible for the plight of Islam is its totalitarian nature. In fact, it can be regarded as the first totalitarian ideology, for Islam is not just about reading *namaz* and performing *hajj*. As Arun Shourie showed in his book, *The World of Fatwas: Or the Shariah in Action*, Islam seeks to govern each and every aspect of human life. It is not only things such as the ultimate reality, soul, and morality that Islam is bothered about. It also informs the believers how animals should be slaughtered, what position should be taken during sexual intercourse with one's wife, and how one should urinate. It is true that other religions, too, intend to comprehensively control the lives of their adherents—control over daily chores through rituals, shaping of habits and customs by popular discourses, influencing everyday behavior through the notions of purity and pollution.

But only Islamic theologians of repute argue at length and write copious texts on the most trivial matters. Shourie writes:

> May a mother spread paper on the floor so that the child may defecate on it rather than soil the floor, and so that the excreta may be thrown away that much more easily? Not quite a religious question, you would think. But that is only because we have not yet grasped the basic claim of Islam, nor have we got to know the *Ulema* . . . .
>
> May one sleep on leg resting on the other knee? Again not a momentous question exactly, not quite the question one would think of as a religious one.

Instances multiply, as Shourie has shown: Does intercourse break the fast even if there is no ejaculation? Does using a tooth paste break the fast? Islamic scholars of great learning deliberate at length on such issues, and come out with recondite arguments to justify their verdicts. Islam does not leave anything to chance; like a stern master who wants total control over his servants, Islam wants to control each and every aspect of the life of the faithful. Not many scholars of Islam lay much emphasis on an important fact of this religion: that, literally, Islam means "submission". And submission it is to the Book, the other sacred texts, and their interpretations. Total submission. Openness is clearly an alien concept in Islamic society, for such a society is essentially totalitarian. And for this very reason Islam is inherently antithetical to open societies.

As for the totalizing effect of a Leftist vision, one only has to look at the Soviet Union, China, and other such regimes. As Kristol wrote in his memoirs, *Reflections of a Neoconservative*, thinking stops in such countries. He rightly pointed out that communist regimes did not produce even a decent Marxist philosopher; all of them—Lukacs and Gramsci, Habermas and Adorno—thrived in Western countries. Further, Kristol said, the works of Leftist writers and artists are banned in communist societies: the books of Sartre were never published in the erstwhile Soviet Union, nor were the plays of Brecht performed or the paintings of Picasso exhibited. In fact, anything of any merit in the Soviet Union was quickly banned and banished. Solzhenstein and Pasternak are the more prominent examples.

In other words, whenever there is an endeavor, especially state-sponsored endeavor, to achieve any "version of the good life and the good society", the consequences are unpleasant. It is indeed ironical that Kristol, who so brilliantly portrayed the spiritual malaise and intellectual desertification in communist countries, should argue in favor of the conscious and state-dependent efforts to bring realize the good life and the good society. For such efforts encroach upon the autonomy of the society and culture.

As American conservative thinker Frank S Mayer wrote:

> [C]ommunity conceived as a principle of social order prior and superior to the individual person, can justify any oppression of individual persons so long as it is carried out in the name of "community", or of its agent, the state.
>
> This is the principle of collectivism, and it remains the principle of collectivism even though the New Conservatives who speak of "community" would prefer a congeries of communities based upon locality, occupation, belief, caste, class, traditional ties, to the totalizing and equalizing national or international community which is the goal of the collectivists.

Whatsoever be the nature of collectivism—Rightwing or Leftwing, conservative or progressive, nationalist or radical, small or big—the consequences are not only unpleasant but also mostly end up further empowering government; it assumes the role of the inquisitor and the arbiter in the process. When it is not censorship, it is a public outcry for ban or violent demonstrations. And who will decide whether or not to ban? Some clique of politicians or bureaucrats who invariably have their own agendas, vested interests, and idiosyncrasies.

Demands of censorship and ban on various works of fiction and art are rooted in the postulate that there do exist *blueprints* for society, art, literature, and culture—and not just some *version* of the good life and the good society; the obscene and the objectionable are those expressions, forms, and discourses which do not conform to the well-established canons and generally accepted norms. Needless to say, it is the collectivities such as political parties, community, socio-cultural organizations, or the most powerful institution, the state, that determine the legitimate and the illegitimate, the sober and the obscene, the progressive and the regressive.

Now it is one thing to respect the age-old traditions and conventions of society: this is the proper conservative position. It leads to skepticism for any drastic change and downright disdain for any change that is for its own sake. However, it is quite an-

other thing to accept a jaundiced vision about society as the *real* society, and guard it doggedly (This is the problem with Islam). Such an attitude leads to reaction, for what differentiates conservatism from reaction is the fact while the conservative is opposed to drastic, unnatural change that is imposed by force, the reactionary is opposed to *any* change.

In fact, a healthy respect for traditions and conventions is not in consonance with any vision, for such a vision will always tamper with the age-old traditions and conventions, infringing upon their autonomy in one way or the other. *Laissez faire* should be as much a social policy as it should be the economic theory of conservatism.

This brings us to the third strand of conservatism: limited government. The economy can remain free and the society open only if the government is small, its powers are limited, and its role is restricted to the traditional duties—viz., maintaining law and order, running the administration, protecting the borders, foreign affairs, etc. Whenever government grabs powers to intervene in the economy or society, trouble begins. This is the reason why all totalitarian societies—communist, fascist, or Islamic—have been proved to be comprehensive failures. The ones that have not collapsed are bound to sooner or later.

For when a government determines to run the country in accordance with "some version of the good life and the good society", that version plays havoc with the autonomy of the traditions and conventions of the society. Similarly, when the government tries to regulate and control the economy to achieve some grand objectives like social justice, removal of poverty, or rapid industrialization, it ends up strangulating entrepreneurship and arresting growth. This is evident from the economic history of India since Independence. Myriad crimes have been committed in the name of grand objectives. It would not be incorrect to say that the absence or weakening of any one of the three strands of open society, free market, and limited government would lead to the weakening of individual liberty.

As mentioned earlier, the chasm between the Orient and the Occident is often exaggerated. Almost every Western thinker or scholar is of the opinion that individual liberty is an alien concept to India. Even an author-philosopher of the stature of Albert Camus, who can hardly be accused of racial or imperialist bias, wrote in *The Rebel*:

> It is obvious that a Hindu pariah, an Inca warrior, a primitive native of Central Africa, and a member of one of the first Christian communities had quite different conceptions about rebellion . . . In other words, the problem of rebellion only seems to assume a precise meaning within the confines of Western thought . . . . The problem of revolt, therefore, has no meaning outside our Occidental society. It would be tempting to say that it was relative to the development of individualism . . . .

This view is true to a certain extent, for the concept of individual liberty was perfected—as a social policy, an economic principle, and a political reality—primarily in the Anglo-Saxon world. However, it would be wrong to say that the concept of individual liberty was unheard of in our country. In this context, it is instructive to note that in all major philosophical schools of India, save certain Buddhist sects, the path to salvation is through individual effort. A visit to any temple would make it clear that individualism is deeply rooted in the Hindu psyche: a Hindu would like his name to be mentioned on a brick even if he had donated a most insignificant amount to the temple.

As for traditional Hindu canons of statecraft, it may be noted that what concerned the authors of various *Dharmashastras* was the protection of *dharma*; they never produced any roadmaps for any utopia; they were bothered about what *is*, and not what *ought* to be. They were the upholders of order, not dreamers or visionaries. Visions are dangerous when political philosophers have them; more than 100 million died under various communist regimes in the twentieth century; millions were slaughtered by Hitler's thugs in order to create a master race. As A. L. Basham wrote in *The Wonder That Was India*, "the texts [on politics] do not discuss

wholly impossible utopias." None of the great Hindu authors on polity, be it Kautilya or Manu, could be accused of social engineering, of creating a new society or a new man. Such concepts have remained alien to traditional India. Which is in sharp contrast to the intellectual history of the West. Right from the beginning, utopia and social engineering have been an integral part of its intellectual discourse, Plato's *Republic* being the most prominent example. Not surprisingly, *Manusmriti* and French conservative Maistre agree on the glory of coercive authority. Says the great law-giver of India, "Where the Rod [*danda*] moves about, black and with red eyes, destroying evil, there the subjects do not get confused, as long as the inflictor sees well." For Maistre, "all grandeur, all power, all subordination rest on the executioner... Take away this incomprehensible agent and at that moment, order will give way to chaos, thrones will fall and society will disappear." Manu and Maistre, both practical men.

What this shows is that Indian conservatism is inherent and unspoken. In fact, Indian conservatism—based on individual liberty and focusing on open society, free market, and limited government—will not only be in tune with the traditions, conventions, and intellectual history of the country but also allow them to grow in a healthy manner. The alternative is a cesspool—the cesspool of Swadeshi, obscurantism, and cretinism.

Unfortunately, the supposedly Rightwing organizations such as the Sangh Parivar have chosen the rotten alternative. The consequence is that the Left continues to dominate public discourse; intellectuals and liberals end up assisting the Left.

The tragedy of India is not just that liberals do not get mugged by reality but also that even the so-called Rightists—the Sangh Parivar and its associates—carefully avoid any contact with reality. The nation is doomed unless a sizeable part of its illuminati embrace conservatism wholeheartedly.

16 How to Check Intellectuals

Sahitya Sangeeta Kala Bihinah
Sakshyat Pashu Puchha Bishanahinah;
Trinang Na Khadannapi Jeevamana-
Stad Bhagdheyang Param Pashunam.

Without literature, music, and art,
a man is like a tailless beast.
Though we cannot eat leaf and grass like animals,
we would live in society as a great beast.
— Bharttruhari, a Sanskrit poet

Democracy is much more than voting once in a while. It is about making governance and policy responsible and responsive to the people, and not just to a bunch of loud civil society representatives and NGO activists.

Democracy is the matrix from which our freedoms emanate; it should also be the shield against all tyrannies, great as well as petty. In the ultimate analysis, this matrix of democracy is about people. If people are sober, discerning, and rational, democracy is safe. But if people are reduced to a rabble of atomized entities, animated only by the vicissitudes of emotions, it is not. Unfortunately, this is the case today in India.

Gladiatorial Disposition

We, the people of India, are increasingly becoming incapable of equanimity and poise. A cricket match is won, and Dhoni and his men become gods; a match is lost a couple of days later, they become demons. In both cases, emotions get the better of us, making us forget that the cricketers are not gods or demons but men, and men succeed and fail. The disposition is generally gladiatorial. In public life, major events like, say, the Nirbhaya rape, unleash a great deal of claptrap and sanctimony which cause a lot of heat but no light. In politics and society, Left-leaning activists peddle sentimentalism to further their dangerous agenda. In economy, they promote their discredited theories.

All these things happen primarily because philistinism is rampant in Indian society. Owing to widespread ignorance about politics, society, economics, history, and science, Left-libbers dominate public discourse: people's ignorance is blissful for them. The situation can be rectified only by infusing vitality and vibrancy in society, equanimity and poise in life, and reason in public discourse. General refinement is the need of the hour.

Genuine scholars, philanthropists, educationists and well-meaning individuals ought to work to enhance refinement in life. The process has to start right at the beginning—that is, at school and home when the child is impressionable—and become a part of life. It is not that there is no realization about the value of culture; we tend to hold people of taste in high-esteem. For instance, when looking for a spouse, money and status are not the only parameters; people also expect etiquette and social graces.

General refinement, however, is not something that can happen by government fiat, legislative action or wishful thinking; it is a gradual process. When the process gathers steam, much of Left-wing mendacity and theatrics will vanish anyway.

The Role of Cognoscenti

At the same time, one can't wait till society enriches and ennobles itself. Men and women of heightened consciousness will have to

take on the intellectuals. They need to scrutinize intellectuals. This can only be done by blasting to smithereens the Leftist theories, doctrines, ideas, and ideals. This will be a non-violent war in which scholarship will be the main weapon and disdain for anything Leftwing the attitude. It will be a war in which no quarter should be given.

For too long, the Left has been mollycoddled by liberals and even liberalizers; for too long, the pigheadedness and cantankerousness of commies and their fellow travelers have been tolerated; for too long, their ideas have been given undue deference. All in the hope that these folks would see reason or at least listen to the other side. In this context, I would like to narrate an incident.

In the run-up to the 1999 general election, the Confederation of Indian Industry (CII) organized meetings with important political parties to inform them of the beneficial nature of market economy. As a business journalist, I covered the Confederation's interaction with Left leaders. A prominent economist apprised the communists about the abysmal human development indices and how liberalization could help improve the situation. I still remember a term he used—"litany of woes"—to describe the plight of the poor. The communists sullenly heard the prominent economist's arguments—and then unleashed their rhetoric against him, the CII and India Inc.

Two aspects of the meeting were striking: first, the Left's reaction, which was doctrinaire, almost Pavlovian; and, second, the prominent economist's obsequious pleadings with the communists to seek their approval for liberalization. His supplication was: look, we don't believe in your ideology but we concede that its goals are laudable; and, by the way, these are also our goals. Since the economic philosophy we believe in actually helps achieve your goals such as poverty eradication, please appreciate the efficacy of the market economy.

This incident has allegorical significance because our liberalizers have been pleading with Left-wing economists and intellectuals to accept, or at least not oppose, economic reforms since 1991. Capitalism—or, at any rate, some aspects of it—can be beneficial

for all sections of society, including workers and peasants. This is the sum and substance of their message to their "Leftist friends." The latter, however, disdainfully rebuff such entreaties. The liberalizer proposes, the Leftist intellectual disposes.

But how does it matter? The Left has been politically isolated and electorally battered; it does not appear a big player in any possible political configuration in the foreseeable future. So, why worry about them and their cantankerousness?

Marketplace of Ideas

It needs to be understood that the Left's influence has always been greatly disproportionate to its political strength. For the marketplace of ideas is curiously egalitarian in more than one sense of the word. Social and economic equality obviously attracts a huge premium. More importantly, what matters in the public discourse is the ability of the participants to promote their ideas, not their political muscle. It's a level-playing field. And it is here that the Left gains an upper hand.

It is a well-known fact that the official Left—the two communist parties (CPI and CPM)—has better human material than other groups. Communist leaders are much better than their counterparts in other parties in terms of integrity and intellect. They don't follow power blindly; they focus on influence on policy instead. Their views also have more consistency than those of the leaders of other parties. This helps pinkish intellectuals to peddle Leftist ideas. Low self-esteem of India's Economic Right also helps make such Leftist ideas as inclusion, social justice, and empowerment popular, for these ideas are accepted unquestioningly rather than analyzed critically.

Certain things need to be given utmost importance in the war against intellectuals. First, as I just mentioned, it is impossible to convince communists and their fellow travelers about the validity of any view that is in dissonance with their ideology. Never ever have they accepted either the genuineness of the opinions of others or the inadequacies, let alone complete erroneousness, of their

own philosophy. So, there cannot be any dialectic with them. They have erected a wall around themselves in which there are no windows. They are the prisoners of their ideology; but the funny part is that they think that the rest of the world is in prison. It makes no sense trying to have a meaningful dialogue with them; so if you can't convince them, crush them.

Secondly, we should be skeptical about anything they say or propose. We have to remember that anything that is repugnant to reason, as commonsense, and decency is a Leftwing cause. I follow a simple principle: I consider whatever intellectuals say is wrong unless proven otherwise. I fail to recall when they were correct. In fact, I regard them as my beacon in a perverse sense: I look for the stand of intellectuals on the issues I don't comprehend properly or am not interested in. Then I know that the opposite stand is correct!

Ad hominem Attacks

Thirdly, we have to prepare armor against *ad hominem* attacks. As mentioned in earlier chapters, *argumentum ad hominem* is favorite weapon of intellectuals. It is also the favorite weapon of dirigiste politicians, the biggest instance being the proliferation of reservation in the country after Mandal. The ever-rising demand for the expansion of the scope of quotas is rarely opposed by politicians because they fear being branded as anti-poor. Where to get the armor from?

For this, we have to examine the credulity and cowardice of liberalizers. They believe in their heart of hearts that the Left is sincerely interested in the uplift of the poor, equally opportunity, etc. This is incorrect. In fact, the Left wants to transform the world in such a way that it conforms to the theories taught by Marx, Engels, Lenin, and other apostles. Eradication of poverty, egalitarianism, etc., are not the ends; they are the means to capture power, gain influence, and eliminate any rival way of thinking. A few million human lives mean nothing to them if they are convinced about the correctness of their path. Whether it was the

collectivization drive in Stalin's Russia, Mao's experiments in China, or Pol Pot's murderous legions in Cambodia, what has always mattered is ideology.

If liberalizers just turn their basic premise—that Leftists have their heart in the right place—upside-down, they would be able to launch a counter-attack. One just has to remind Left-leaning intellectuals and communists that the ideology they prefer was responsible, among other things, for the death of over One hundred million people all over the world in the twentieth century. This will take care of the *ad hominem* assaults from their side. It needs to be mentioned here that recalling the wrongdoings of communism and socialism does not amount to an *ad hominem* strike.

Cultural life has to be rejuvenated and the leading lights of society ought to be more assertive against intellectuals. Equally, if not more, important is the support from big business. The captains of industry have to champion the cause of economic liberty and democracy. Tycoons cannot take capitalism—the only system which allows and thrives in freedom—for granted. No system can continue without the sustainability of its philosophical and ideological underpinnings. You cannot have X-ism in a country where the climate of opinion is positively anti-X-ism. This is exactly the case in India. While the economic policy is getting farther from Nehruvian socialism, public discourse is still conducted in a patently Leftist idiom. This is because the opinion-making apparatus is still in the hands of Left-leaning intellectuals.

Industrialists have the money but not the cerebral acumen or human material to win the hearts and minds of people for capitalism. Even many key editors of media houses owned by big capitalists are socialists at heart and make it evident in their work. It would not be an exaggeration to say that India's industrialists have little say in molding public discourse and, consequently, the policy framework. Of course, they are powerful enough to get their work done from the government, but they rarely influence the people at large with their opinions.

This is unlike the scene in the United States where there are dozens of conservative and libertarian think-tanks, whose endow-

ments run in billions of dollars and which do solid research in all areas. All these institutions are the result of philanthropy of big business as well as ordinary people.

Enlightened Self-interest

Consider the case of the American Enterprise Institute (AEI). In the 1940s, it was just another industry body called the American Enterprise Association. Over the years, it grew into a premier Rightwing think-tank. Similarly, other well-endowed conservative and libertarians foundations came into being. Which is not surprising given that fact often big businesspersons donate much of their fortune to charities, foundations, etc., for the betterment of mankind and for enlightened self-interest.

On the other hand, big industrialists in India are generally unaware of the concept of enlightened self-interest. Most of them are typical Hindus, for whom the world revolves around their businesses, family, inheritance, and so on. Beyond that, there is personal glory—awards in the name of the patriarch, participation jamborees organized by media houses in which the captains of industry rub shoulders with the powers that be, recognition by government by way of Padma Shri and Padma Bhushan, and so on. And there is *Moksha*, for which they patronize religious activities. Seldom do they become joiners in the system for the defence of liberty, economic or otherwise, for this could be risky since an active public figure attracts a lot of scrutiny.

It needs to be mentioned here that the Swatantra Party, the only Indian political party that promoted the cause of the Economic Right, did not receive enthusiastic support from the country's businessmen. Eventually, the party, founded by the noted statesman C. Rajagopalachari or Rajaji, ceased to exist in 1974, within two years after his death. In *Rajaji: A Life*, Rajmohan Gandhi talked about the lack of funds, "which galled all the more in the context of Nehru's well-publicized charge that Swatantra was 'the rich man's party.' CR and his colleagues vigorously advocated a ban on company donations to political parties, but Nehru rejected

the suggestion: almost all the contributions were going to Congress. In addition, Nehru asserted that he would reject any gifts from a company that also gave money to the Swatantra. Moreover, in a crucial comment, Ghanshyamdas Birla declared, 'Swatantra politics were not good businessmen's politics'." So much for the enlightened self-interest of India's business tycoons.

According to Rajmohan Gandhi, "Most companies became too frightened to give anything to Swatantra. The ones contributing also gave, in almost every case, a much bigger sum to Congress—but, despite Nehru's assertion, no money was in fact returned by Congress."

It is time India Inc. redeemed itself and meaningfully helped the champions of liberty by setting up think-tanks, publications, media houses, etc., for the promotion of liberty. There is no point in lamenting the waywardness of government policy, the perversity of public discourse, and the anti-business biases of India's intellectuals. Big business has to do something to change the situation.

In a nutshell, Indian society has to undergo a benign metamorphosis, the people of heightened consciousness have to wage a war against pinkish intellectuals, and industry has to aid and encourage both efforts. The alternative is intellectuals' unrelenting jihad against growth, prosperity, and reason.

Index